First World War
and Army of Occupation
War Diary
France, Belgium and Germany

51 DIVISION
154 Infantry Brigade
Seaforth Highlanders
(Ross-shire Buffs, the Duke of Albany's)
4th Battalion
1 January 1916 - 31 March 1918

WO95/2888/1

The Naval & Military Press Ltd
www.nmarchive.com
Published in association with The National Archives

Published by

The Naval & Military Press Ltd

Unit 10 Ridgewood Industrial Park,

Uckfield, East Sussex,

TN22 5QE England

Tel: +44 (0) 1825 749494

www.naval-military-press.com

www.nmarchive.com

This diary has been reprinted in facsimile from the original. Any imperfections are inevitably reproduced and the quality may fall short of modern type and cartographic standards.

© Crown Copyright
Images reproduced by permission of The National Archives, London, England, 2015.

Contents

Document type	Place/Title	Date From	Date To
Heading	WO95/2888/1 4 Battalion Seaforth Highlanders		
Heading	51st Division 154th Infy Bde 1-4th Seaforth Hdrs Jan 1916-Feb 1919 From Meerut Div Dehradun Bde		
Heading	1/4 Seaforth Hdrs Jan Vol. IV 6.1.6 Transferred From 46th Bde 15C Div to 15 4th Bde. 51st Div.		
War Diary		01/01/1916	31/01/1916
Heading	154th Bde 1/4th Bn. Seaforth Highlanders (T.F.) War Diary 1/2/16-29/2/16 Vol V		
War Diary	Cardonette	01/02/1916	07/02/1916
War Diary	La Neuville.	08/02/1916	29/02/1916
Heading	1/4th Seaforth Highrs War Diary for Period 1st-31st March 1916 Vol VI		
War Diary		01/03/1916	31/03/1916
Heading	1/4 Seaforth Hrs Vol VII		
War Diary	Etrun	01/04/1916	02/04/1916
War Diary	Trenches L 1	03/04/1916	08/04/1916
War Diary	Ecurie	09/04/1916	14/04/1916
War Diary	Trenches L 1	15/04/1916	20/04/1916
War Diary	Etrun	21/04/1916	26/04/1916
War Diary	Trenches L 1	27/04/1916	02/05/1916
War Diary	Ecurie	03/05/1916	09/05/1916
War Diary	Trenches L	10/05/1916	15/05/1916
War Diary	Etrun	16/05/1916	20/05/1916
War Diary	Trenches L	21/05/1916	28/05/1916
War Diary	Ecurie	29/05/1916	31/05/1916
Heading	1/4th Battalion Seaforth Highlanders War Diary Period 1st-30th June 1916 Vol 9		
War Diary	Ecurie	01/06/1916	02/06/1916
War Diary	Trenches L 1	03/06/1916	09/06/1916
War Diary	Etrun	10/06/1916	14/06/1916
War Diary	Trenches L 1	15/06/1916	20/06/1916
War Diary	Ecurie Defences	21/06/1916	30/06/1916
Heading	154th Brigade. 51st Division. 1/4th Battalion Seaforth Highlanders. July 1916		
Heading	War Diary of 1/4th Bn Seaforth Highrs From 1st July 1916 to 31st July 1916 (Volume 10)		
War Diary	L. Right I Sub Sector	01/07/1916	04/07/1916
War Diary	Etrun	05/07/1916	09/07/1916
War Diary	L Right I. Sub Sector	10/07/1916	13/07/1916
War Diary	Lovez	14/07/1916	14/07/1916
War Diary	Villers Brulin	15/07/1916	15/07/1916
War Diary	Le Souich.	16/07/1916	16/07/1916
War Diary	Prouville.	17/07/1916	20/07/1916
War Diary	Meaulte	21/07/1916	21/07/1916
War Diary	S 15"C D	22/07/1916	23/07/1916
War Diary	High Wood.	24/07/1916	26/07/1916
War Diary	Meaulte.	27/07/1916	31/07/1916
Heading	154th Brigade. 51st Division. 1/4th Battalion The Seaforth Highlanders. August 1916		
War Diary	Fricourt Wood	01/08/1916	05/08/1916

War Diary	Dernacourt	06/08/1916	08/08/1916
War Diary	Liercourt	09/08/1916	10/08/1916
War Diary	Ebblinghem	11/08/1916	13/08/1916
War Diary	Armentieres.	14/08/1916	15/08/1916
War Diary	Trenches	16/08/1916	19/08/1916
War Diary	Subsidiary Line	21/08/1916	25/08/1916
War Diary	Baillieul	26/08/1916	31/08/1916
Heading	War Diary of 1/4th Battn Seaforth Highlanders From 1st September 1916 to 30th September 1916 (Volume 12)		
War Diary	Bailleul	01/09/1916	01/09/1916
War Diary	Romarin	02/09/1916	02/09/1916
War Diary	Trenches	03/09/1916	07/09/1916
War Diary	Armentieres	08/09/1916	14/09/1916
War Diary	Trenches	15/09/1916	21/09/1916
War Diary	Erquinghem	22/09/1916	24/09/1916
War Diary	Estaires	25/09/1916	29/09/1916
War Diary	Candas	30/09/1916	30/09/1916
Heading	War Diary of 1/4th Battn Seaforth Highrs. From 1at October 1916 to 31st October 1916 (Volume 13)		
War Diary	Candas	01/10/1916	02/10/1916
War Diary	Sarton	03/10/1916	03/10/1916
War Diary	Bus-Les Artois	04/10/1916	04/10/1916
War Diary	Courcelles	05/10/1916	07/10/1916
War Diary	Colin Camp	08/10/1916	11/10/1916
War Diary	Louvencourt	12/10/1916	16/10/1916
War Diary	Raincheval	17/10/1916	17/10/1916
War Diary	Lealvillers	18/10/1916	25/10/1916
War Diary	Trenches	26/10/1916	29/10/1916
War Diary	Lealvillers	30/10/1916	31/10/1916
War Diary	War Diary of 1/4th Battn Seaforth Highlanders. From 1/11/16 to 30/11/16 (Vol 26)		
War Diary	Lealvillers	01/11/1916	05/11/1916
War Diary	Mailly Wood	06/11/1916	07/11/1916
War Diary	Trenches.	08/11/1916	12/11/1916
War Diary	Forceville	13/11/1916	13/11/1916
War Diary	Mailly. Wood E	13/11/1916	15/11/1916
War Diary	Trenches	15/11/1916	19/11/1916
War Diary	Mailly. Wood	20/11/1916	23/11/1916
War Diary	Varennes	24/11/1916	24/11/1916
War Diary	Puchevillers	25/11/1916	25/11/1916
War Diary	Aveluy	26/11/1916	30/11/1916
Heading	4th Seaforth Highlanders. War Diary From 1.12.16 to 31.12.16 Vol 15		
War Diary	Near Aveluy.	01/12/1916	02/12/1916
War Diary	Wolfe Huts	03/12/1916	06/12/1916
War Diary	Trenches	07/12/1916	08/12/1916
War Diary	Huts.	09/12/1916	10/12/1916
War Diary	Bouzincourt	11/12/1916	15/12/1916
War Diary	Ovillers Huts.	16/12/1916	22/12/1916
War Diary	Trenches	23/12/1916	26/12/1916
War Diary	Huts	27/12/1916	29/12/1916
War Diary	Bouzincourt	30/12/1916	31/12/1916
Heading	War Diary of 1/4th Battn Seaforth Highlanders Volume 28 From 1st January 1917 to 31st January 1917		
War Diary	In The Field	01/01/1917	31/01/1917
Map	Trench Map 51B N.W. 2		

Heading	War Diary of 1/4th Seaforth Highlanders (Volume 29) from 1st February 1917 to 28th February 1917		
War Diary	Favieres	01/02/1917	04/02/1917
War Diary	Forrest L'Abbaye	05/02/1917	05/02/1917
War Diary	Fontaine-Sur-Maye	06/02/1917	06/02/1917
War Diary	Noeux	07/02/1917	07/02/1917
War Diary	Nuncq	08/02/1917	08/02/1917
War Diary	Marquay	09/02/1917	10/02/1917
War Diary	Ecoivres	11/02/1917	20/02/1917
War Diary	Bray Wood	21/02/1917	21/02/1917
War Diary	Trenches Roclincourt	22/02/1917	22/02/1917
War Diary	Trenches	23/02/1917	26/02/1917
War Diary	Maroeuil.	27/02/1917	28/02/1917
Heading	War Diary of 1/4th Battn Seaforth Highlanders from 1st March 1917 to 31st March 1917 (Volume 30)		
War Diary	Maroeuil.	01/03/1917	04/03/1917
War Diary	Maroeuil Wood	05/03/1917	10/03/1917
War Diary	Trenches (Sabliere)	11/03/1917	15/03/1917
War Diary	Ecurie	16/03/1917	22/03/1917
War Diary	Huts In Maroevil Wood	23/03/1917	31/03/1917
Heading	War Diary of 1/4th Battn Seaforth Highlanders (Volume 31) from 1st April 1917 to 30th April 1917		
War Diary	Maroeuil Wood	01/04/1917	03/04/1917
War Diary	Ecurie	04/04/1917	07/04/1917
War Diary	Front Line	08/04/1917	08/04/1917
War Diary	A.22.b.3.3 to A.23.a.4.2 Sheet 51B N.18.1 1/10000	08/04/1917	08/04/1917
War Diary	Front Line See Previous	09/04/1917	11/04/1917
War Diary	Larasset	12/04/1917	15/04/1917
War Diary	St Laurent Blangy	16/04/1917	22/04/1917
War Diary	Fampoux	23/04/1917	24/04/1917
War Diary	Arras	25/04/1917	25/04/1917
War Diary	Maisieres	26/04/1917	30/04/1917
Heading	War Diary of 1/4th Battalion Seaforth Highlanders (Volume 32) from 1st May 1917 to 31st May 1917		
War Diary	Maisieres	01/05/1917	12/05/1917
War Diary	Y. Huts Etrun	13/05/1917	14/05/1917
War Diary	Arras.	15/05/1917	16/05/1917
War Diary	Front Line E. of. Roeux	17/05/1917	20/05/1917
War Diary	Railway Embankment H.13.d. Ref. Map 51 B.N.W.	21/05/1917	28/05/1917
War Diary	Support Line W.of Roeux	29/05/1917	31/05/1917
Heading	War Diary of 1/4 Battn Seaforth Highrs Volume 33 from 1st June 1917 to 30th June 1917		
War Diary	Arras	01/06/1917	01/06/1917
War Diary	Bailleul	02/06/1917	03/06/1917
War Diary	Valhuon	04/06/1917	04/06/1917
War Diary	Lisbourg	05/06/1917	06/06/1917
War Diary	La. Panne	07/06/1917	21/06/1917
War Diary	Lederzeele	22/06/1917	30/06/1917
Heading	War Diary of 4th Battn. Seaforth Highlanders (Volume 34) from 1st July 1917. to 31st July 1917		
War Diary	Lederzeele	01/07/1917	08/07/1917
War Diary	E Camp Near Poperinghe A 30	09/07/1917	09/07/1917
War Diary	Trenches	10/07/1917	11/07/1917
War Diary	'E' Camp A 30 Central	12/07/1917	12/07/1917
War Diary	Houtkerque	13/07/1917	21/07/1917
War Diary	Windmill Camp (A 17 d)	22/07/1917	31/07/1917

Type	Description	From	To
Heading	War Diary of 1/4th Battalion Seaforth Highlanders (Volume 35) from 1st August 1917 to 31st August 1917		
War Diary	Yser Canal Bank	01/08/1917	01/08/1917
War Diary	Front Line Trenches South of Langemarck.	02/08/1917	04/08/1917
War Diary	Yser Canal Bank.	05/08/1917	05/08/1917
War Diary	Huts A 30 Central (Sheet 28 N.W.)	06/08/1917	07/08/1917
War Diary	'N" Camp St. Janster Biezen	08/08/1917	09/08/1917
War Diary	Helvelinghem	10/08/1917	22/08/1917
War Diary	Camp St. Janster Biezen.	23/08/1917	28/08/1917
War Diary	Murat Camp	29/08/1917	31/08/1917
Heading	War Diary of 1/4th Battn Seaforth Highlanders Volume 36 from 1st September 1917. to 30th September 1917		
War Diary	Murat Camp	01/09/1917	03/09/1917
War Diary	Dirty Bucket Camp (Ref. Map Sheet 28. N.W.)	04/09/1917	05/09/1917
War Diary	Front Line Trenches Near Langemarck	06/09/1917	08/09/1917
War Diary	Yser Canal Bank	09/09/1917	11/09/1917
War Diary	Siege Camp	12/09/1917	18/09/1917
War Diary	Assembly Positions	19/09/1917	19/09/1917
War Diary	West of Langemarck	20/09/1917	21/09/1917
War Diary	Siege Camp	22/09/1917	23/09/1917
War Diary	Poperinghe	24/09/1917	28/09/1917
War Diary	Courcelles	29/09/1917	30/09/1917
Heading	War Diary of 4th Bn. Seaforth Highlanders (Volume 37) From 1st October 1917 to 31st. October 1917		
War Diary	Courcelles Le. Comte	01/10/1917	04/10/1917
War Diary	Front Line Trenches N.W. of Guemappe	05/10/1917	07/10/1917
War Diary	Front Line	08/10/1917	12/10/1917
War Diary	Carlisle Huts	13/10/1917	20/10/1917
War Diary	Front Line Trenches	21/10/1917	27/10/1917
War Diary	Izel-Les Hameaux	28/10/1917	31/10/1917
Heading	154th Brigade. 51st Division. 4th Battalion Seaforth Highlanders November 1917		
Heading	War Diary of 4th. Battalion Seaforth Highlanders. (Volume 38) From 1st. November 1917. to 30th. November 1917. Vol 26		
War Diary	Izel-Le Hameaux	01/11/1917	16/11/1917
War Diary	Bapaume	17/11/1917	17/11/1917
War Diary	Lechelle	18/11/1917	19/11/1917
War Diary	Metz	20/11/1917	24/11/1917
War Diary	Ribemont	25/11/1917	30/11/1917
Heading	4th. Battalion Seaforth Highlanders. Narrative of Operations From November 20th. to November 22nd. 1917.		
Miscellaneous	4th. Battn. Seaforth Highlanders. Narrative of Operations From November 20th. Till November 22nd.		
Map Miscellaneous	Moeuvres Ed 5F 1/20.000		
Miscellaneous	Medical.		
Miscellaneous	Cavalry.		
Miscellaneous			
Map Miscellaneous	Map to accompany Operations for & by 4 Seaforth		
Heading	1/4th Bn. Seaforth Highlanders War Diary from 1st December 1917. to 31st December 1917 Vol. 39		
War Diary	Bapaume.	01/12/1917	01/12/1917
War Diary	Bertincourt	02/12/1917	02/12/1917

War Diary	In The Trenches	03/12/1917	04/12/1917
War Diary	Fremicourt	05/12/1917	15/12/1917
War Diary	In The Front Line Trenches	16/12/1917	22/12/1917
War Diary	Bancourt	23/12/1917	27/12/1917
War Diary	Lebucquiere	28/12/1917	31/12/1917
Heading	War Diary of 1/4th Battn. Seaforth Highlanders Volume 40 from 1st January to 31st January 1918 Vol 28		
War Diary	Lebucquiere	01/01/1918	14/01/1918
War Diary	Front Line Trenches Demicourt.	15/01/1918	17/01/1918
War Diary	Fremicourt.	18/01/1918	18/01/1918
War Diary	Courcelles Le Comte.	19/01/1918	19/01/1918
War Diary	Bellacourt	20/01/1918	31/01/1918
Heading	War Diary of 1/4th Battn Seaforth Highrs Volume 41 from 1st February 1918 to 28th February 1918 Vol 12		
War Diary	Bellacourt	01/02/1918	01/02/1918
War Diary	Ritz Camp Near Achiet Le. Grand	02/02/1918	09/02/1918
War Diary	Log East Wood Ablainzeville	10/02/1918	12/02/1918
War Diary	Lebucquiere	13/02/1918	19/02/1918
War Diary	Front Line Trenches N.W. of Demicourt	20/02/1918	28/02/1918
Heading	51st Division. 154th Infantry Brigade. War Diary 1/4th Battalion The Seaforth Highlanders March 1918		
Heading	War Diary of 1/4th Battn Seaforth Highlanders Volume 42 from 1st March 1918 to 31st March 1918		
War Diary	Front Line Trenches N.W. of Demicourt	01/03/1918	05/03/1918
War Diary	Lebucquiere	06/03/1918	09/03/1918
War Diary	Front Line Trenches N.W. of Demicourt	10/03/1918	14/03/1918
War Diary	Lebucquiere	15/03/1918	21/03/1918
War Diary	Beaumetz-Morchies Line	22/03/1918	24/03/1918
War Diary	N.E. of Bapaume-Peronne Rd. About N. 5 b.	24/03/1918	25/03/1918
War Diary	Warlencourt Eaucourt	25/03/1918	25/03/1918
War Diary	Sailly Au Bois	26/03/1918	26/03/1918
War Diary	Barly	27/03/1918	28/03/1918
War Diary	Busnettes	29/03/1918	31/03/1918

WO95/2888/1

4 Battalion Seaforth Highlanders

51ST DIVISION
154TH INFY BDE

1-4TH SEAFORTH HDRS
JAN 1916- FEB 1919

FROM MEERUT DIV
DEHRA DUN BDE

1/4 Seaford Mrs

Jan / Vol IV

154/51

6.1.16 Transferred from 46th Bde 15th Div.
to 15 of Bde, 5th Div.

18 S.
5 Shield

WAR DIARY or INTELLIGENCE SUMMARY

Army Form C. 2118.

Place	Date	Hour	Summary of Events and Information	Remarks and references to Appendices
	1-1-16		New Year's Day. No parades were held. The men of the Battalion were entertained to dinner by the Officers. The dinner was served in various estaminets in Burbure, and each was visited by Capt. Goode & the Chaplain, who both addressed the men and wished them the compliments of the season. In the evening a smoker was held in the schoolroom.	
	2-1-16		Church Parades were held in the schools at various hours. In the afternoon route marches were held by Companies.	
	3-1-16		Battalion again took part in a Brigade Route March in a manner similar to the previous one.	
	4-1-16		To-day the C.O. inspected the Billets. Company Books were also inspected. In the afternoon a lecture on map-reading was given to all junior officers by the acting Adjutant, a lecture also by Sergt/Major to N.C.O's on Discipline etc. The transport took part in a Brigade Transport Route March.	
	5-1-16		Marching order inspection by Coy information for the following days trek.	
	6-1-16		To-day we leave the 46th Div'd 15th Division, and thereunto attached to the 154th Bde 51st (Highland) Division T.F. This new Division is our original one to which we were attached in Burbure. Battalion fell in at 11-15am and entrained at Bellinn for Amiens area. After a train journey of about 10 hours – pretty well uneventful the Battalion marched 6 miles to billets at Cardonette ( ) and arrived there at 1.30 a.m. We have been lucky in joining this Division while out on rest, and we shall probably be here some weeks before again going in action.	
	7-1-16		Cleaning up generally. Cardonette as a rest area is very poor. Our one consolation is that we are not far from Amiens, to which the men may perhaps be permitted to visit. Billets are very poor.	
	8-1-16		Ammunition and equipment inspection by Companies.	
	9-1-16		Church parade was held to-day in a field near H.Q. Coys Billet.	

WAR DIARY or INTELLIGENCE SUMMARY

Army Form C. 2118.

Instructions regarding War Diaries and Intelligence Summaries are contained in F. S. Regs., Part II. and the Staff Manual respectively. Title pages will be prepared in manuscript.

(Erase heading not required.)

Place	Date	Hour	Summary of Events and Information	Remarks and references to Appendices
	10-1-16		Inspection of helmets, goggles etc. and training in bayonet drill and bombing of arms etc. under Coy. arrangements.	
	11-1-16		Battalion was inspected to-day by Brig. Gen. Stewart R.J. addressed the Battalion. He addressed the men, and hoped that after inspecting the Battalion our future movements would merit greater similar to that we have realised for past achievements. We have constructed a rifle range, and this is to be used for testing rifles, and firing with Zeiss to Silent.	
	12-1-16		Battalion route march was held in the afternoon, and afternoon, a Football match was held in the afternoon, Burnspears having the 5th Black Watch, although putting up a good fight, were had to retire defeated by 2–1. Command of the Battn was taken over to-day by Capt. L.D. Henderson at his return from hospital. Coys engaged in drill as names for programme.	
	13-1-16		A small fatigue party was furnished for work with R.E. under 2/Lt. J. Mackie. The Adjutant, Capt. Gordon, went on leave, and his duties were temporarily taken over by 2/Lt. J. Mackie.	
	14-1-16		To-day the Brig. General inspected Companies at work.	
	15-1-16		C.O. inspected Billets. Church parade held.	2 O.R.C. Lance Corp. Battalion
	16-1-16		Battalion route march. In the afternoon a Football match between Batt. and 4th Black Watch. Again ended by 1–0.	
	17-1-16		Battalion paraded at 8 de Rutenburg ground. A detail of 40 men per Coy was furnished, and proceeded to Angouleur.	
	18-1-16		Battalion engaged in digging at Entrenching ground. Another Football match against 40th Camerons walked again in our favour by 3–1.	
	20-1-16		Digging as usual at Bar entrenching ground.	

WAR DIARY or INTELLIGENCE SUMMARY

Army Form C. 2118.

Place	Date	Hour	Summary of Events and Information	Remarks and references to Appendices
	21-1-16		Digging as usual. Weather continues dry but cold.	
	22-1-16		Digging continued. A Football match between Batt. + Bde M.G. Coy resulted in a win for Batt. by 3-0.	
	23-1-16		Church Parade was held in a field near H.Q.	
	24-1-16		Digging continued. Lecture by M.O. to Coy officers on water hygiene.	
	25-1-16		The Batt. was inspected to-day by the G.O.C. 51st Divn, Major General Harper. Batt. formed up in mass formation in a field north of the village. He inspected closely all Coys, but made no remarks. A failure of the inspection was the turning of the men on parade.	
	26-1-16		A scheme of manœuvres is commencing to-day and we are supposed to be part of a force occupying the reserve trenches at Carnoustie. An active part was taken to-day in the manœuvres. We occupied the trenches at Carnoustie. Battalion were in outpost line and when the hostile attack was made (held by 4th Camerons) called for reinforcements. The Battalion advanced splendidly in open order, and successfully assisted to repel the hostile attack.	2nd Lt A.M. McDonald joined to-day
	27-1-16		Digging continued. Lectures by M.O. to Companies.	
	28-1-16		Coys had to shift tents owing to another Batt. arriving in Carnoustie. 6th Seaforths + Batt. resulted in our defeat by 4-1.	2/Lt A.M. Sharp joins Battn
	29-1-16		Football match between	
	30-1-16		Church Parade held in Football field.	2/Lt H. Fellows 2/Lt C. Drummond joined Batt.
	31-1-16		Coys engaged in morning at Grenade throwing, Rifle range, and digging. In the afternoon close-order drill, and handling of arms.	

154th B'd'e

1/4th Bn. Seaforth Highlanders (T.F)

War Diary

1/2/16 – 29/2/16.

Vol V

Army Form C. 2118

WAR DIARY
or
INTELLIGENCE SUMMARY
(Erase heading not required.)

Instructions regarding War Diaries and Intelligence Summaries are contained in F. S. Regs., Part II. and the Staff Manual respectively. Title Pages will be prepared in manuscript.

Place	Date	Hour	Summary of Events and Information	Remarks and references to Appendices
Cardonette	1/2/16		Baths at Rainneville were allotted to Coys. in batches of 20 at a time. In the afternoon a football match between H.Q. Battalion and the 8th Devons resulted in a win for us by 3–0.	2 Lt. H.O. Zillwood 2 Lt. C.H. Emery joined Batt. today
	2/2/16		A Brigade Route March was held today on the usual lines.	
	3/2/16		A Field Day. Operations were carried out on a large scale, and the use of smoke candles added a spice of realism to the work. It was quite an interesting day.	
	4/2/16		Various parades were held by Coys.	
	5/2/16		Coys. engaged in morning at digging & grenade throwing. Football match between the Battn. officers & the officers of the Canadian R.R. game resulted in a decisive win for us by 5–1. It was a most enjoyable game, and full of laughable incidents.	
	6/2/16		Church Parade was held on the football field.	
	7/2/16		The Brigade still is today in a fresh area. Battn. fell in at 9.50 a.m. and marched to La Neuville sur Corbie, a distance of 8 miles. Considering the bad roads, marching was very good, and we arrived at 1.30 p.m. Billets here are very good.	
La Neuville	8/2/16		Parades were held today under Coy. arrangements.	
	9/2/16		Parades as previous day. A party of men the Lt. travisid as scouts paraded under the R.S.M. for instruction.	
	10/2/16		Companies at Grenade throwing and rifle range.	
	11/2/16		Parades as on previous day.	
	12/2/16		Brigade was engaged in tactical exercises, in which Battn. took part.	
	13/2/16		Church Parades on usual lines, with the exception that Presbyterian service was held under Brigade arrangements.	
	14/2/16		Companies engaged in drill under their own arrangements.	
	15/2/16		Companies at drill similar to previous day.	

WAR DIARY
or
INTELLIGENCE SUMMARY
(Erase heading not required.)

Army Form C. 2118

Instructions regarding War Diaries and Intelligence Summaries are contained in F. S. Regs., Part II. and the Staff Manual respectively. Title Pages will be prepared in manuscript.

Place	Date	Hour	Summary of Events and Information	Remarks and references to Appendices
La Neuville	16/2/16		A fatigue party of 100 men supplied by Battalion for railway work under R.E.'s. The preliminary rounds of a Brigade Boxing Tournament were held in the evening at Corbie.	
	17/2/16		Baths at La Neuville are allotted to Batts. The arrangements have an appreciable and a good supply of clothing is at hand. The finals of the Boxing tournament arranged for the Battalion 4 victories, and also the prize for dancing. The Brig. General was present and made a few remarks.	
	18/2/16		Companies went today engaged at Bombing.	
	19/2/16		Companies at bombing, and at anti-gas practice. A football match against 4th Bedfords ended in our defeat by 1-0.	
	20/2/16		Church Parades were held as on previous Sunday. Capt. C.G. Hogg 66.O.R.	Capt. C.G. Hogg arrived today, and were posted to Coys. Capt. C.G. Hogg assumed command of the Battalion vice Capt. R.S. H. Moncrieff.	from Battn. today.
	21/2/16		Companies engaged at bombing, and rifle practice.	
	22/2/16		Close extended order drill by Coys. also helmet inspections.	
	23/2/16		Baths at La Neuville allotted to men of last week's fatigue party. Companies engaged at drill under their own arrangements.	
	24/2/16		Baths again at disposal of Battn. Company parades as on previous day. Companies at Bombing and rifle range.	
	25/2/16		Battn. Route march in morning. Feet inspection in the afternoon. Snow commenced to fall very heavily about evening.	
	26/2/16		Church Parades were held today in the Recreation Room, owing to the snow. A number	
	27/2/16		Medical inspection was held afterwards by M.O.	

Army Form C. 2118

WAR DIARY
or
INTELLIGENCE SUMMARY
(Erase heading not required.)

Instructions regarding War Diaries and Intelligence Summaries are contained in F.S. Regs., Part II. and the Staff Manual respectively. Title Pages will be prepared in manuscript.

Place	Date	Hour	Summary of Events and Information	Remarks and references to Appendices
La Teuville	28/2/16		Companies at Bombing and Helmet drill. Two 3rd Coys held kit inspections in the afternoon. Shrapnel Helmets were issued to-day.	
	29/2/16		The Division commences its move to-day to a final area. Battn moved off at 11am on the first days trek. The march was a very stiff one, as the roads were in a very bad condition. We arrived at Harmieux at 3pm and billeted there for the night. Lt. Col. C.H. Campbell D.S.O. (Cameron Hrs.) from the command of 12th Bn. W. Yorks Regt. has arrived, and taken over command.	

C.N. Campbell Lt Col
1/4 Seaforth Hrs
Comm'dg.
29/2/16.

1/4th SEAFORTH HIGHrs

War Diary

for

Period 1st — 31st March 1916

Vol VI

WAR DIARY or INTELLIGENCE SUMMARY

(Erase heading not required.)

Army Form C. 2118

Instructions regarding War Diaries and Intelligence Summaries are contained in F. S. Regs., Part II. and the Staff Manual respectively. Title Pages will be prepared in manuscript.

Place	Date	Hour	Summary of Events and Information	Remarks and references to Appendices
	1/3/16		Beautiful day. March has not been continued as originally intended.	
	2/3/16		Weather continues splendid at Dieuvaux. Companies engaged at drill and short route marches. Our defaulters was again put forward.	
	3/3/16		Battalion moved off at 10.30 a.m. and marched to Rubempré a distance of 1 mile and accomodation here is much better.	
	4/3/16		Owing to bad stormy weather parade arranged were cancelled.	
	5/3/16		Church parades were held by Companies. Companies also had a short route march.	
	6/3/16		Battalion moved on today to Doullens. A splendid march and good roads. We arrived at 3 p.m. and found good billets.	
	7/3/16		The day was spent in cleaning up generally and short route marches by Companies.	
	8/3/16		Battalion moved today at 8.30 a.m. to Beauquesne. Roads were very heavy and cut up which hindered our transport. We put up here for the night.	
	9/3/16		Again on the move to Louvencourt. This was a very long march about 16 miles, a hot dinner was supplied half way on the road. All the Companies were billeted in a large factory. Parties of men visited the trenches in the morning in order to act as guides for the Battalion. The Lewis Gunners and Signallers went up early in the morning. At 9 p.m. the Battalion moved off to the trenches by companies and relieved the 138th Regiment of the 23rd French Division. On our right are the 1st Devons of the 5th Division & on our left the 7th Argyll & Sutherland Highlanders. Nos. 1 and 2 Companies were in the firing line and supports and Nos. 3 and 4 Companies in reserve. Everything the during time the trenches are very good.	

WAR DIARY or INTELLIGENCE SUMMARY

Army Form C. 2118

(Erase heading not required.)

Place	Date	Hour	Summary of Events and Information	Remarks and references to Appendices
	11/3/16		Weather very good. Day was quiet except for some bombing by the enemy. We had one man wounded in the morning, our artillery strafed the enemy lines in the afternoon turning fire of about 8 rounds near the water supplying place. We had two or three lightly wounded by bullets. No 2 Company bagged a stern doubling across the open. Weather continues fine.	
	12/3/16			
	13/3/16		Beautiful day and very quiet. Company changed over positions in the evening and after which dawning. He had only been with the Battalion 14 days. He was a grand type of soldier and his fine personality will be missed by all ranks. Our Adjutant Captain Gordon returned from a months course at IIIrd Army School. temporary command of the Battalion was assumed by Major J.W. McIntosh, 4th Gordon Highlanders. 2nd Lieut. Mackie relinquished the temporary adjutancy.	
	14/3/16			
	15/3/16		Fine day but dull. Some heavy shells fell in our reserve line. We had 1 killed & 1 wounded. Afternoon quiet. Day was dull but day, nothing much doing. Battalion was relieved at night by 10th Gordons. Nos. 3 & 4 Coys came back to dug-outs at Almè Central and lay in support to 4th Gordons. Nos. 1 & 2 went to villam in town village and No. 2 Coy to dug-outs further behind	
	16/3/16			
	17/3/16		Battalion in Brigade Reserve. Quiet day and nothing eventful took place.	
	18/3/16		Fine weather. Nothing much doing	
	19/3/16		Weather continues fine. Nothing of importance happened.	
	20/3/16		Rather dull day. Our aeroplanes were rather active.	
	21/3/16		Day very dull & very quiet.	
	22/3/16		Dull drizzling day and very quiet. We relieved the 11th Gordons in the front line in the evening Nos. 3 and 4 Coys and portion of Divisional Cyclists took over the front line and Nos. 1 and 2 Companies and portion of Divisional Cyclists were in support.	

WAR DIARY
or
INTELLIGENCE SUMMARY
(Erase heading not required.)

Army Form C. 2118

Instructions regarding War Diaries and Intelligence Summaries are contained in F. S. Regs., Part II. and the Staff Manual respectively. Title Pages will be prepared in manuscript.

Place	Date	Hour	Summary of Events and Information	Remarks and references to Appendices
	23/3/16		Dull day and fairly quiet. Germans made grenade attack on our left on left of Brigade on our left from 1 p.m. till 1.15 p.m. the left was maintained by aid of Stokes and 2 inch Mortars. We gained the upper hand. Our grenadiers threw over 1000 grenades.	
	24/3/16		Snowfell in the early morning and weather was very cold all day. Day was quiet. No. 4 Coy sniper hit a German & also another who came to bring him in.	
	25/3/16		Weather continues very cold and wet. The enemy bombed the right sap of No. 4 Coy at stand to this morning. Febo bombs were thrown which fell short and our bombers replied with rather a little brighter. Enemy snipers and artillery fairly active. The enemy swept over support line parapet with machine gun fire at 11 p.m. and 2 a.m.	
	26/3/16		Dull day. Enemy artillery shelled our front and support line at intervals during day. Our artillery retaliated. Two of our men had to be evacuated suffering from shellshock.	
	27/3/16		Weather cold and dull. Enemy artillery active. We had three Lewis Gunners slightly wounded by a shell striking their emplacement. The battalion was relieved from the trenches in the evening by the 4/5th Gordon Highlanders and marched by companies to billets in Etrun. Weather bright but still cold. The day was devoted to cleaning up.	
	29/3/16		Beautiful sunny day. No. 1 Company went to the Baths here. A fatigue party of 150 was supplied by the Battalion for the sulphur of Trenches.	
	30/3/16		Fine weather. Baths were allotted to No. 2 Company. A working party of 150 men was supplied the same as yesterday. A draft of 144 other ranks arrived from England.	

57

1/4 Seaforth Hos

Vol VII.

16 Sep

WAR DIARY or INTELLIGENCE SUMMARY

(Erase heading not required.)

Army Form C. 2118

Place	Date	Hour	Summary of Events and Information	Remarks and references to Appendices
Etrun	1/4/16		Battalion in rest at Etrun. Beautiful weather. No 3 Coy & Headquarters went to Baths. A working party of 150 men was supplied for supplying of trenches, the remainder were at drill. The Drafts were drilled under Sergeant Major. Commanding Officer inspected No 3 Company.	
	2/4/16		The Weather continues good. No 4 Company went to Baths. The same working party was supplied as yesterday. Church Parade. Weather very warm.	
Trenches L1	3/4/16		Battalion relieved 4th Gordons in the trenches on L1 sub-sector in the evening. No 1 & 2 Companies in the firing line & Nos. 3 & 4 Companies in Reserve. The C.O. inflicted No 4 Company on the left of the Argylls.	
	4/4/16		The night was quiet except for some bombing which blew in part of communication trench. A dull day but sharp hostile artillery fairly active. Enemy bombed our Left front & support line but eased on our artillery opening fire. 1st Wilts relieved 1st Cheshires on our right. Day was quiet.	
	5/4/16		Dull weather. Day was quiet except for some hostile shelling. Casualties 1 man wounded.	
	6/4/16		Sunny & cold, some light shells near our Hqrs & Headquarters. No 3 & 4 Companies relieved No 1 & 2 Coys in firing line.	
	7/4/16		Dull & very. Artillery active on both sides. There was a violent explosion to our right at 10.30 p.m. followed by an artillery bombardment.	
	8/4/16		Weather bright but cold. Artillery active on both sides. 2nd Lt Mills assumed preparations for the making of a new trench behind Germain lines & at 10 pm this was bombarded by our artillery with good results.	
Ecurie	9/4/16		Beautiful day. Our own & hostile artillery active. The 4th Gordons relieved the Battalion in the evening. No 1 Coy & No 9 & 10 Lewis Gunners went to billets in ETRUN, No 2 Coy in reserve at ARRI CENTRALE & Headquarters and Nos. 3 & 4 Companies near ECURIE in dug-outs.	
	10/4/16		Weather very good. No 1 Coy supplied party of 80 men for supply of trenches on new No 2 Coy, 60 men under O.C. L1 sub-sector, Nos 3 & 4 Coys 80 men each under R.E., constructing defences of ECURIE.	
	11/4/16		Day was very wet & cold. Fatigue parties were supplied the same as yesterday.	
	12/4/16		Weather cold and wet. Usual parties supplied as on previous days.	

WAR DIARY
or
INTELLIGENCE SUMMARY
(Erase heading not required.)

Army Form C. 2118

Instructions regarding War Diaries and Intelligence Summaries are contained in F. S. Regs., Part II. and the Staff Manual respectively. Title Pages will be prepared in manuscript.

Place	Date	Hour	Summary of Events and Information	Remarks and references to Appendices
ECURIE	13/4/16		Day was cold with occasional showers. Fatigue parties supplied as on previous days. A few shells landed near Headquarters.	
	14/4/16		Weather changeable and cold. Usual working parties supplied. Lieut Powell & 2nd Lt Robertson joined Battalion from England.	
Tranchée L1	15/4/16		Changeable weather. A draft of 180 joined Companies. The Battalion relieved the 4th Gordons on 21 Feb night. No 1 & 2 Coys in firing line and Nos 3 & 4 Coys in Reserve. 2nd Lieuts on our right and 9th Argylls on left. Major R.A. Stewart, 9.1.0., 1st Bayrsths arrived and took over command of the Battalion.	
	16/4/16		Weather dry but cold. Enemy artillery and trench mortars active. Trenches were improved and deepened.	
	17/4/16		Day wet & cold 9 Trenches becoming muddy. Hostile trench mortars active. An enemy patrol of three was dispersed by rifle fire. Work continued. Relaying & improving trenches. Casualties, 1 man still shock. Day wet and trenches in a bad state. Intermittent shelling and trench mortars by enemy. Our gun retaliated. Enemy shelled the nation dump at 8.30 pm & 9.30 pm. after Survey returned from Base duty No 3 & 4 Companies relieved No 1 & 2 Coys in firing line. Casualties two men wounded by bomb.	
	18/4/16		Day was wet & cold. Hostile artillery and trench mortars active. Heavy bombardment of enemy trenches continued	
	19/4/16		Showery weather. Enemy artillery sent over more shells than usual. Our Trench mortars were active in the afternoon. Repairing of trenches continued. Casualties, 1 man wounded.	
	20/4/16		Showery weather. Enemy artillery fairly active. Battalion was relieved by 4th London & went to billets at ETRUN at MAROEUIL. Battalion went for baths	
ETRUN	21/4/16		Day very wet. A fatigue party of 100 men was supplied for R.E. work at MAROEUIL. Day was devoted to cleaning up.	
	22/4/16		Bright sunny day. Church Parades were held under Battalion arrangements. No. 3 & 4 Coys supplied 100 men each for work on Brigade Grounds.	
	23/4/16		Beautiful weather. The G.O.C. Brigade presented Medal ribbons at a parade held at HAUTE AVESNES and after at R.E. Stores MAROEUIL.	
	24/4/16		Fine and cool. Was issued. 4 Officers and 130 men attended Divisional Theatre. 100 men were supplied for work at Divisional Grenade School and 100 men at R.E. Stores MAROEUIL.	
	25/4/16		Good weather. Parades under Company arrangements including tube helmet drill. Officers instructed in Lewis Gun work. 100 men were supplied for work at MAROEUIL.	

WAR DIARY
or
INTELLIGENCE SUMMARY
(Erase heading not required.)

Army Form C. 2118

Place	Date	Hour	Summary of Events and Information	Remarks and references to Appendices
ETRUN	26/4/16		Very warm weather. Parade under Company arrangements. No 2 & 4 Coys were instructed in use of Lewis Gun. Lieut. Finch gave a lecture to Officers and N.C.Os on precautions against gas. Fatigue party of 100 men worked on Brigade Grenade Ground.	
Tranchée L1	27/4/16		Wood weather. Battalion relieved 4th Gordons in trenches. No 3 & 4 Coys in front line and No 1 & 2 Coys in reserve. The 1st Gordons are on our right and 9th Argylls on the left.	
	28/4/16		At 2 a.m. an enemy mine was sprung on our left and our front line and dugouts heavily shelled by artillery and trench mortars damaging our trenches in several places and blowing in part of communication trench. Our artillery vigorously retaliated. Damaged parts were repaired & cleared. Casualties. 11 men wounded.	
	29/4/16		Enemy bombarded our line with trench mortars for an hour at 8.20 am. An enemy aeroplane was brought down behind our lines. Our artillery sent alert and claim to have hit a Hun. In the evening enemy shelled our front line but did little damage. Work was carried on clearing & repairing trenches and building new traverses and dug-outs. Casualties. 1 killed. 2 wounded.	
	30/4/16		Bright sunny day. Enemy artillery shelled our front line at 10 am but did little damage. Our guns were active during the day. An enemy trench & support line doing considerable damage. Trench mortars were active on both sides. Wire was put up in front of sap. Parts of our front lines were filled in with boards wire & trenches were cleaned and repaired.	

4.5.16

ABS Stewart Lt Colonel.
Comdg: 1/4 Seaforth Highlanders

WAR DIARY or INTELLIGENCE SUMMARY

Army Form C. 2118

1/4 Seaforth — Vol 8

Place	Date	Hour	Summary of Events and Information	Remarks and references to Appendices
Trenches L1	1/5/16		Day was quiet except for an artillery scheme carried out by our guns. Our grenadiers fired over 100 rifle grenades. Our snipers were also active claiming 5 certain hits. Gas was reported from R.2 sector and precautions were taken but it proved a false alarm. Work was continued building traverses retaining trench. Casualties 3 wounded.	
	2/5/16		Good weather. Artillery & trench mortars active on both sides. Our grenadiers were also active firing a number of rifle grenades to which enemy retaliated. Usual work on trenches continued. Casualties 6 wounded by rifle grenades. Quiet day. Battalion was relieved by 4th Gordon Hrs, No 4 Coy to Hrs, No 1 & 2 Coys to Luna trenches & 8 suppollon going to billet in Etrun. Headquarters.	
Ecurie	3/5/16			
	4/5/16		Very warm day. No 3 Company relieved Gordons to trench 9 No 3 Coy to Abri Central. Remainder of Battalion supplied a fatigue party of 60 men for L.2. bill sector and 1 platoon for L.2. Platoon supplied a fatigue party for work under R.E. constructing defences of Ecurie. Casualties 2 wounded.	
	5/5/16		Good weather. The usual fatigue parties were supplied.	
	6/5/16		Weather continues very good. Usual fatigues as on previous day.	
	7/5/16		Beautiful day. Fatigue parties supplied as on previous days.	
	8/5/16		Good weather. Usual fatigues supplied by battalion.	
	9/5/16		Dry wet & cold. Battalion relieved 4th Gordons in L.1. Sub sector. No 1 & 2 Coys in front line and No 3 & 4 Companies in support. The 9th Argylls rejoins our left and 14th Royal Warwicks on our right. Casualties 1 wounded.	
Trenches L	10/5/16		Bright sunny day. Enemy artillery & trench mortars active doing some damage to our trench. Work was carried on cleaning & repairing trenches & laying our trench boards. Our Lewis guns fired at hostile working parties & ammunition trucks.	
	11/5/16		Good weather. Bombing activity on both sides 9 casual shelling. Usual work continued rebuilding ramparts & wiring round the redo. A patrol went out to the crater in front of Rap 2.3 but returned on being fired on.	
	12/5/16		Fine weather. The enemy trenches to our right were heavily shelled between 10 and 11 am doing a lot of damage and their guns retaliated on our trenches. Enemy sent a large number of shells into Anger between 2 and 4 pm presumably searching for our batteries. Usual work continued repairing trenches.	
	13/5/16		Very quiet & cold. During trench mortar & artillery faintly active. Usual work cleaning & repairing trenches carried on.	
	14/5/16		Weather continues cold & wet. Our grenadiers fired about 50 rifle grenades with good effect, otherwise day very quiet. Repairing & cleaning up of trenches was carried on.	
	15/5/16		Very wet weather. Quiet day. Battalion was relieved by 4th Gordons & went back to billet in Etrun.	

Army Form C. 2118

WAR DIARY
or
INTELLIGENCE SUMMARY
(Erase heading not required.)

Instructions regarding War Diaries and Intelligence Summaries are contained in F.S. Regs, Part II. and the Staff Manual respectively. Title Pages will be prepared in manuscript.

Place	Date	Hour	Summary of Events and Information	Remarks and references to Appendices
ETRUN	16/5/16		Weather very good. The day was devoted to cleaning up.	
	17/5/16		Bright during weather. Battalion went to Divisional Baths at MAROEUIL. Company paraded under Commanding Officer and inspected all billets.	
	18/5/16		Commanding Officer inspected all billets. Parades held under Company arrangements. Bombers of No 3 Coy were instructed by Battn. Bombing Officer. The men of new draft paraded under Regimental Sergeant Major.	
	19/5/16		Beautiful day. Parades held under Company arrangements. A draft for instruction in use of Short Rifle	
	20/5/16		Weather bright & very warm. Parades as for previous days	
	21/5/16		Voluntary Church Parades under Battalion arrangements. Battalion relieved 4th Gordons and 9th Royal Scots in No 1 Sector.	
Trenches L	22/5/16		Enemy artillery quieter than usual but their trench mortars were active doing some damage to our trenches. Many bombardment to our right during the night. An officer patrol went out and heard Germans working. Work was carried on improving trenches. Casualties 1 wounded.	
	23/5/16		Good weather. Naval shelling. Enemy trench mortars active on our left front. Our Commanding Officer Lt. Col. A V St. Stewart DSO, who killed by a piece of trench mortar bomb while going round the the Battalion will be missed by all ranks. Casualties 1 officer killed.	
	24/5/16		Enemy trench mortars very active sending over bombs all day. Our retaliation did not check them. Usual work done on trenches, wiring etc. Casualties 5 wounded	
	25/5/16		Naval activity by enemy artillery & trench mortars a large number of whizz-bangs being fired at front line. At 2.30 am enemy made a demonstration at Sap 24 throwing many hand grenades. Our bombers on the sap retaliated but no attempt was made to attack the sap & everything became quiet on our field guns retaliating. Enemy artillery & trench mortars were very active during the day. Work rebuilding trenches continued. Casualties 1 wounded.	
	26/5/16		Good weather. Mutual bombing & shelling by enemy to which our guns retaliated. Major Wathanh of the 10th Durham Light Infantry arrived and took over command of the Battalion. Casualties 4 wounded.	

1875 Wt. W593/826 1,000,000 4/15 J.B.C. & A. A.D.S.S./Forms/C. 2118.

WAR DIARY
or
INTELLIGENCE SUMMARY
(Erase heading not required.)

Army Form C. 2118

Place	Date	Hour	Summary of Events and Information	Remarks and references to Appendices
Tuardis L	28/5/16		Our trench mortars fired a number of rounds at 12 midnight. At 1:15 am a mine went up beyond our left flank. Heavy artillery fire was opened on our strong left but little damage was done. Our artillery vigorously replied and put up a barrage infront of enemy trenches. There was great activity by artillery, trench mortars & machine gun for an hour but it gradually quietened down. At 4.30 am enemy shelled R.H.Q. LA SABLIERE doing some damage. Battalion was relieved by 4th. Gordons, No 1 Coy going to reserve at Lenthen Road, No 2 Coy to trench No 3 to Blue Centrale & No 4 Coy to Abri Mouton. R.H.Q at Ennui. Casualties 1 wounded.	
Ecurie	29/5/16		Beautiful day. Battalion supplied fatigue parties for work under R.E. constructing dugouts, wiring & improving defences of Ennui.	
	30/5/16		Good weather. Usual fatigue parties. No 2 Company went to Baths at Anzin.	
	31/5/16		Very warm weather. Usual fatigues supplied. Coms of No 2 Company & Headquarters went to Baths at Anzin. 2nd Lieuts Harrop, Burnham, Jackson & Phillips arrived from England and were posted to Companies. Enemy sent a number of shells near the dump & Headquarters.	

A.D. Henderson Capt
1/4th. Seaforth Highrs.

1/4th Battalion
Seaforth Highlanders

War Diary

Period

1st - 30th June 1916.

WAR DIARY or INTELLIGENCE SUMMARY

Army Form C. 2118

Place	Date	Hour	Summary of Events and Information	Remarks and references to Appendices
Faumes	1/6/16		Good weather. Fatigue parties supplied for work under R.E. Our aeroplanes active. Heavy bombardment some way to our left about 8.30 p.m. Everything quiet on our sector.	
	2/6/16		Bright sunny day. Our aeroplanes again active. Usual fatigue parties supplied. Day very quiet.	
Trenches L.1	3/6/16		Very warm weather. Battn. relieved 4th Gordons on L1 subsector, Nos. 3 & 4 bays in front line 9/200 1 & 2 bays in support, 7th Argylls on our left & 2 R. West Kents on our right. A German tried to come over to our lines bearing a white flag but was killed by the enemy before reaching our trenches. Hostile trench mortar active. Casualties 2 killed, 1 wounded.	
	4/6/16		Day quiet in our sector. Some distance to our right, after heavy artillery fire for 3 hours, enemy opened 3 mines at 9 p.m., followed by intense bombardment & continued till 10.30 p.m. Work done. Usual shelling & sniping. Communication trenches and wiring to left of L.1 & C. Casualties nil.	
	5/6/16		Usual shelling & bombing on both sides. The large enemy trench mortar was active today. Repairing of trenches continued. Casualties 1 wounded.	
	6/6/16		Enemy artillery & trench mortars active doing some damage to our trenches. Our guns retaliated. Our snipers claim to have hit a German. Repairing of damaged trenches carried out. Casualties 1 Officer wounded.	
	7/6/16		Wet, changeable weather. Quiet day except for slight shelling & trench mortars. It was reported that the enemy had taken up part of the wire & precautions were taken in case of attack but nothing took place. Trenches repairs & wiring continued. Casualties 2 men wounded. Dull. Quiet.	
	8/6/16		Enemy artillery & trench mortars very active. Our right front Bay & Chemin Creux were heavily shelled. We retaliated. Two patrols went out at night to examine Germans wire. One patrol heard sounds as of enemy putting their wire and also found an old disused trench. The German wire was reported thin & irregular. Repairs carried on in damaged trenches. Casualties 2 men killed & 6 wounded.	
	9/6/16		Good day & fairly quiet. Usual shelling. Casualties nil. 1st King's Liverpool Reserve Battalion joined Battalion as escort or [?] command. Casualties nil. Major R.J. Hunt	

WAR DIARY
or
INTELLIGENCE SUMMARY
(Erase heading not required).

Place	Date	Hour	Summary of Events and Information	Remarks and references to Appendices
Etrun	10/6/16		Wetday. Day devoted to cleaning up. Nos 3 & 4 coys went to Baths. 12 N.C.O.'s applied for R.E. & other fatigues. New Battalion Mess Room opened for Battalion in Reserve at Etrun.	
	11/6/16		Wet day. Church Parade held under Battalion arrangements. No.1 Coy & Hd. Qrs. went to Baths. 96 O.R.'s were on various fatigues for R.E.'s etc.	
	12/6/16		Wet day. Parades under Coy arrangements. 284 men applied for various fatigues.	
	13/6/16		Day cold & wet. 84 men on fatigues. Major Hunt inspected No. 3 Coy. A fatigue Coy composed of bombers from each Coy was formed under 2t Pender.	
	14/6/16		Day windy & cold. Parades under Coy arrangements. 68 men applied for fatigues.	
Trenches L 1	15/6/16		Army day but cold. Battn. relieved 4th Yorks in Trenches. Nos 1 & 2 Coys in front line & Nos 3 & 4 Coys in Lichfort. Night very quiet.	
	16/6/16		Day dry but dull. & fairly quiet except for shelling by enemy howers at Chenin Camp & Bellicturn Trench. & cleaning of trenches carried on. Casualties nil	
	17/6/16		Good day. Enemy artillery & Trench mortars active causing some casualties & damaging our trenches. That about activity. Six enemy aeroplanes passed over our lines. Repairing & cleaning of trenches continued.	4 killed 3 wounded
	18/6/16		Good weather. Enemy artillery & Trench mortars active. Eight German aeroplanes crossed over our lines at 3.15 p.m. & again at 8 p.m. A British aeroplane was forced to land in front of German lines after an aerial combat & a man was seen to walk from it into German lines. Another aeroplane fell behind THELUS. Two Germans were captured by us at Sap. 20, one of whom was wounded. They apparently deserted.	
	19/6/16		Work done repairing & cleaning trenches & wiring. Casualties 1 man killed 9 1 wounded.	
	20/6/16		Good day & fairly quiet except for some shelling. Two patrols went out getting within 20 yards of German line & heard work going on. Repairing & wiring of trenches continued. Casualties 2 men wounded. Bright day. Mutual bombing, shelling & work done repairing trenches. Casualties 1 man killed & 2 wounded.	

WAR DIARY or INTELLIGENCE SUMMARY

Army Form C. 2118

Place	Date	Hour	Summary of Events and Information	Remarks and references to Appendices
Essars Estaires	21/6/16		Very fairly quiet. Battalion was relieved by 4th Gordons & went into reserve. No 1 Coy. to Euston Road, No 2 Coy. to Cairn, No 3 Coy. to Albe Central & No 4 Coy. to Abri Moulton & H.Q. to Beuvry a platoon of Bombers to each Coy. Casualties nil.	
	22/6/16		Fine weather. At 3 a.m. the Brigade Bomb Store at Rolencourt was blown up. One of our men who was borrowing was killed. Day good. Aeroplanes active. Returning of dug-outs & wiring carried out.	
	23/6/16		Changeable weather. Our artillery active. Major B.E.P Monro joined Battalion from England.	
	24/6/16		Changeable weather. Our artillery again active. Work done cleaning trenches & wiring. Some of our aeroplanes attacked German Observation Balloons & one balloon burst in flames & fell.	
	25/6/16		Dull day. Our artillery shelled enemy front & support trenches. Work on dug outs continued.	
	26/6/16		Dull weather. Our artillery were very active & intermittently bombarded German trenches. Casualties 4 wounded.	
	27/6/16		Artillery activity continued, our guns bombarding the enemy trenches several times during day.	
	28/6/16		Battalion relieved 4th Gordons in trenches in L1 Sub-sector in the evening. Night was quiet. At "Stand to" the German artillery opened fire on our front trenches & shelled heavily for over half an hour, damaging our trenches & causing some casualties. At 3 p.m. our artillery heavily bombarded German Front Line trenches & our men set off smoke candles, machine guns & trench mortars also co-operating. The German trenches were again bombarded at 4 p.m. with good results, their trenches being badly damaged. Two patrols went out at 11 P.M. reading German wire & front went going on. Casualties 1 killed 9.6 wounded.	
	29/6/16		Bright day. Fairly quiet. Some of our platoon relieved by 2/3/21 st London Regiment who are in for instruction.	
	30/6/16		Our aeroplanes active. Casualties nil.	

A.R.Lundie Lyl
2" Seaforth Highlrs

154th Brigade.
51st Division.

1/4th BATTALION

SEAFORTH HIGHLANDERS.

JULY 1916

Confidential

War Diary
of
1/4th Bn. Seaforth Highlanders

from 1st July 1916 to 31st July 1916.

(Volume 2?)

WAR DIARY or INTELLIGENCE SUMMARY

Army Form C. 2118.

Place	Date	Hour	Summary of Events and Information	Remarks and references to Appendices
L. Riguet 1 Sub-sector	1st	10.50	Quiet day. Occasional shelling. Our aeroplanes active. Enemy strong nerve on our right, followed by heavy bombardment. Snipers claimed 2 hits. Work done retaining trenches.	Yes
	2nd		Quiet Day. Draft of 66 men arrived – Casualties nil.	Yes
	3rd		Quiet Day. Aeroplanes active. Casualties nil.	Yes
	4th		Still day. Heavy rain during night. Relieved in afternoon by 16 London & went into Billets at ETRUN – Snipers claimed 16 Germans during tour. The 1/22 London Regt. was attached to us for instruction during this tour.	Yes
ETRUN	5+6		Rest + baths.	Yes
	7		Co. 2.w to Camp. Supplied working parties of 50 men each.	Yes
	8		Bayonet Horse Show – Battalion 2nd. W.L.	Yes
	9		Church Parade – Officers' Tailors Shop.	Yes
L. Riguet 1 Sub-sector	10		Bn. relieved 16th London Hq. 3rd & 4th Coys in front 1 & 2 in support. K.R.R (14th W.Div) on right, 7th A. & S. Hrs on left. 22nd London Regt. on for instruction.	Yes
	11		1 man slightly wounded. 1 New Lndn. Regt killed. 2 Crews of animals reported enriching trench Pandi. Pri. White Case found out to be Trench from. Man of Draft which arrived in 2nd December whilst bathing at ETRUN.	Yes

WAR DIARY of INTELLIGENCE SUMMARY

Army Form C. 2118.

(Erase heading not required.)

Place	Date	Hour	Summary of Events and Information	Remarks and references to Appendices
	12		Very quiet. No casualties.	yes
	13		Very quiet. Bn relieved by 2/23rd London Regt & returned to "Gibral" in Lousy. No casualties.	yes
LOUEZ	14	9 a.m.	Marched to VILLERS-BRULIN arriving at 2 p.m. About 12 kilometres.	yes
VILLERS-BRULIN	15	4 a.m.	Marched at 4 a.m. to TINCQUES & moved to LE SOUICH.	yes
LE SOUICH	16	6.45 a.m.	Paraded 6.45 a.m. & marched in Brigade to PROUVILLE (24 kilometres)	yes
PROUVILLE	17		Re-Tld. Short march by Companies.	yes
"	18		" " & training.	yes
"	19		" "	yes
"	20	1.30 a.m.	Marched at 1.30 a.m. & entrained at CANDAS, detraining at MARICOURT, marching in Brigade from there to MEAULTE & went into bivouac. A hot & tiring day.	yes
MEAULTE	21		Marched to Reserve Trenches S.15 c & D & relieved 9th H.L.I. Enemy put over a Barrage of Tear Shells but no casualties. Guns A.B.C.D. in road on 152 & 153 R & also here. Weather in Brigade on the same road.	yes

WAR DIARY or INTELLIGENCE SUMMARY

Army Form C. 2118.

Place	Date	Hour	Summary of Events and Information	Remarks and references to Appendices
S.15.c.d	22nd		Artillery active. Informed Trenches & made Shelters.	
	23rd		No 1 & 4 Coys moved up in support of 4th Gordons & HIGH WOOD. No.2 & No 3 & H.Q. B's moved forward to trenches in rear of BAZENTIN-LE-GRAND. The Gordons attacked in early morning. No 1 & 4 Coy suffered severely from shell fire. At 9.30 a.m. No 2 & 3 Coys moved up in advance H.Q. Gordons in HIGH WOOD. No 4 Coy moved in Support Trench & H.Q. 1 moved into trench vacated by No 3 Coy - 1st Argylls on right.	
HIGH WOOD	24th		Weather very warm & made service. No shelling directed on Wood. Enemy Barrage Line just caught Reserve Trench, 200yds in rear of Wood. Constructed a Deepened trench - No 1 & 3 Coys referenced front line of S.15.b.5.10.; on our right & live run along road b.5.10 B.8. joining up with DEVONS. 2d A.S. Hqs on our left. Relief delayed by heavy bombardment by both sides from about 9 p.m. till 11.30 & not complete till just before dawn. A party stood by all night ready to rail German line at S.4.b.3.8. but owing to these unforeseen circumstances it was impossible to have completed post 5.46.35 & pull a preliminary bombardment turning N.W. thence & SWITCH LINE	

2449 Wt. W14957/M90 750,000 1/16 J.B.C. & A. Forms/C.2118/12

Army Form C. 2118.

WAR DIARY / INTELLIGENCE SUMMARY

(Erase heading not required.)

Place	Date	Hour	Summary of Events and Information	Remarks and references to Appendices
HIGH WOOD	25		Line pushed forward during the day to head of 2 or 3 new posts established about 1 about S. 4. C. 8. 8. within 15 feet of German line from which heavy M.G. fire came. An empty concrete M.G. emplacement was occupied without opposition at about S. 4. C. 3. 9, and H.Q. booked up in a post (German) established about S. 4. C. 3. 8. This post came under heavy M.G. fire from 2 guns & also rifle fire, L/Cpl Phillips being killed. There posts were dug, armed & connected up during the night. At 9.20 P.M. after preliminary bombardment M Coy led a rather stormy trench? against N.E. corner of wood. S. 4. d. 9. 8. The attack failed completely, the trench was found heavily manned & apparently untouched by our Artillery fire. The par 5 was greeted with a shower of grenades & a cross fire of M.G. D. Coy. was killed in the fracas – Owing to the number of steel helmets, broken knees & marched in Dug-outs a large number of this various heads, dented & split up. The casualties among the men who took part were very slight – 2 men failed to be accounted for, though the ground was thoroughly searched	

WAR DIARY
INTELLIGENCE SUMMARY

(Erase heading not required.)

Army Form C. 2118.

Place	Date	Hour	Summary of Events and Information	Remarks and references to Appendices
HIGH WOOD	26/4"		Quiet day in wood. Relieved by 9th Bn Black Watch during afternoon & evening. No. 3 Company came under a heavy barrage of gas shells on way out from HAMETZ WOOD & suffered some casualties. Bivouac at HEAULT. Casualties for 5 days — Officers: Killed. Wounded. 2/Lt Ross Captain R.H. Hill. 2/Lt Phillips 2/Lt Clark " M. Lu " Addison (at duty) " Coxen. O.R. Killed Wounded 16 161 Missing 9. 1 Wounded German came in & several wounded from the attack 2 days before others came in & were discovered in the wood. A number of Germans reported buried 77 not including those wounded.	

WAR DIARY
INTELLIGENCE SUMMARY
(Erase heading not required.)

Army Form C. 2118.

Place	Date	Hour	Summary of Events and Information	Remarks and references to Appendices
HEAUTÉ	27		Dist, baths etc: ____	
		30th	Von Brigade Tng. of Bn. on 29th. ____	

G. Urchant p/Col.
Cmdr. 92 a/ Seaforth H'rs.

31/7/16

154th Brigade.
51st Division.

1/4th BATTALION

THE SEAFORTH HIGHLANDERS.

AUGUST 1 9 1 6 ::::::

Army Form C. 2118.

WAR DIARY
or
INTELLIGENCE SUMMARY
(Erase heading not required.)

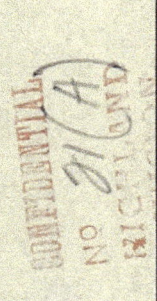

656+

Place	Date	Hour	Summary of Events and Information	Remarks and references to Appendices
FRICOURT WOOD	Aug 1		Battalion went into reserve at FRICOURT WOOD with 3 Coys. & H.Q in wood and 1 Coy in FRICOURT Village. Casualties 2 O.R. wounded. EM	
	2		Very warm day. Battalion at work repairing trenches. EM	
	3		Do. Heavy bombardment by our guns in the evening. Draft of 100 O.R. arrived and joined Companies. EM	
	4		Very warm day. Battalion on fatigue during night digging new communication trench to front line. Heavy shell fire on Bath sides. EM	
	5		Warm day. Fatigue parties supplies to complete new communication trench. Inspecting roads. Casualties - Lt. E.W.P. Finch wounded (slight self injury?) 2 O.R. 4 killed, 13 wounded, 1 missing EM	
DERNACOURT	6		Battalion relieved in afternoon & marched to bivouacs near DERNACOURT. EM	
	7		Cleaning up and Baths. EM	
	8		Company route marches and drill. EM	
LIERCOURT	9		Battalion entrained at MERRICOURT at 8 am. detrained at LONGPRÉ & marched 7 miles to LIERCOURT. EM	
	10		Resting & cleaning up. Bathing in river. EM	
EBBLINGHEM	11		Battalion entrained at LIERCOURT at 9 am. & travelled via ABBEVILLE, ETAPLES & CALAIS arriving at STEENBECQUE at 6.30 pm. Marched to billets near EBBLINGHEM. EM	
	12		Resting & cleaning up. EM	
	13		Church Parade. EM	
ARMENTIERES	14		Battalion entrained at EBBLINGHEM at 10.20 am. & detrained at STEENWERCK at 11.30 am. & marched to billets in ARMENTIERES. EM	

Army Form C. 2118.

WAR DIARY or INTELLIGENCE SUMMARY

(Erase heading not required.)

Instructions regarding War Diaries and Intelligence Summaries are contained in F. S. Regs., Part II. and the Staff Manual respectively. Title Pages will be prepared in manuscript.

6574

Place	Date	Hour	Summary of Events and Information	Remarks and references to Appendices
ARMENTIERES	Aug 16		Enemy shelled ARMENTIERES about 6 pm, wounding 9 of our men & also causing casualties among the A.N.Z.A.C.s and civilians. Relieved a Battalion of 1 N.Z. Brigade in front line trenches. Line very quiet. Bedfords on right & 9th Royal Scots on left. R.14	
TRENCHES	17		Bright day. Line quiet. R.14	
	18		Showery day. Do. Do. Do. R.14	
	19		Enemy shelled ARMENTIERES. Quiet day on our front. R.14	
	20		Battalion at work repairing trenches. Casualties 2 killed & 1 wounded by bomb. R.14	
	21		Wet day. Line quiet. R.14	
Salisbury Line	22		Quiet day. Battalion relieved by 4th Gordons & went into support at Salisbury Line. Draft of 120 arrived. R.14	
	23		Enemy's ammunition by O.C. Coys. Working on improvement of trenches. Fatigue parties supplied for 4th Gordons & R.E.s. R.14	
	24		Good weather. Manual work parties supplied. Boys went to Batn. Draft of 120 posted to Coys. & arrived in line. R.14	
	25		Quiet day. Manual working parties. Enemy shelled Battery positions. Aeroplanes active. R.14	
BAILLEUL	26		Battalion at work on trenches and dug-outs. Artillery & Aeroplanes active on both sides. R.14	
	27		Enemy shelled Square Farm wounding 1 of our men. Battalion relieved by 6th Gordons & marched by Companies to Training Camp near BAILLEUL. Bright day. Church Parade & hit Inspection. R.14	

2449 Wt. W14957/M90 750,000 1/16 J.B.C. & A. Forms/C.2118/12.

Place	Date	Hour	Summary of Events and Information	Remarks and references to Appendices
BAILLEUL	Aug 28		Wet day. Practice inspection of 154th Infy. Brigade by Brigadier. Company drill and training. Draft of 28 O.R. arrived. O.K.	
	29		Showery day. Brigade parade and presentation of Medal Ribbons by General Plumer G.O.C. 2nd Army. No 1015 Sjt. Munro D. No 2 Coy received the Military Medal. Coy drill etc. Pm.	
	30		Wet day. N.C.Os parade under R.S.M. Ram.	
	31		Bright day. Battalion went to Bath at STEENWERCK. Physical training drill, & tading school for Officers Ram.	

J.A. Mulhuskfeld.
Cmdg. 4/Safolk. Rgt.

Si Mitefield
2/9/16 S.

6584
2B

Confidential

War Diary
of
1/4th Battn. Seaforth Highlanders
from 1st September 1916 to 30th September 1916
(Volume ~~24~~)

Army Form C. 2118.

WAR DIARY
INTELLIGENCE SUMMARY

(Erase heading not required.)

660+

Place	Date	Hour	Summary of Events and Information	Remarks and references to Appendices
BAILLEUL	1/9/16		Battalion was in Divisional Reserve near BAILLEUL in Training Camp. Battalion route march & outpost scheme carried out. Cpt M	
ROMARIN	2/9/16		Battalion moved to huts at ROMARIN. Gas alarm was sounded at 11 p.m. but none came in our direction. Cpt M	
TRENCHES	3/9/16		Church parade. Battalion relieved 11th (S) Battn. Northumberland Fusiliers in front line near PLOEGSTEERT. 3 Coys in front line & 1 in support. Cpt M x 9th Royal Scots on right, 1st Camn on left	
	4/9/16		Wet day. Line very quiet. Cpt M	
	5/9/16		Go. Enemy shelled ARMENTIERES. No casualties. 1 wounded. Cpt M	
	6/9/16		Bright Day. Artillery & trench mortars active on both sides. Several enemy aeroplanes came over our lines. One of our aeroplanes was hit by a shell & came down in German lines. Cpt M Work done. Repairing trenches, building dug outs & cleaning trenches. Casualties 3 wounded. Cpt M	
	7/9/16		Bright day. Our aeroplanes active. Repairing of trenches continued. Cpt M	
	8/9/16		Quiet day. Battalion was relieved by 9th Cheshires & proceeded by platoons to old billets in ARMENTIERES. Cpt M	
ARMENTIERES	9/9/16		Battalion supplied 170 men for R.E. fatigues. Part of Battn. went to baths. We relieved 4th Gordons in reserve at ARMENTIERES in billets. Cpt M	
	10/9/16		Battn. supplied 550 men for R.E. fatigue parties carrying gas cylinders. Cpt M	
	11/9/16		Baths. Working parties supplied for R.E. Lt. J. Watt joined Battn. from England. Cpt M	
	12/9/16		Quiet day. Baths. Usual R.E. parties. Cpt M	
	13/9/16		Wet day. Our guns active. Officer training in Bayonet fighting. Cpt M	
	14/9/16		9. (Brig. General L.E. Stuart, commanding 13.4th Infy. Brigade was killed by a shell near 4th Gordon Headquarters at HOUPLINES. Cpt M	

WAR DIARY or INTELLIGENCE SUMMARY

Army Form C. 2118.

Place	Date	Hour	Summary of Events and Information	Remarks and references to Appendices
TRENCHES	15/9/16		Battn. relieved 4th Gordons in front line & No 2 Coy in Support. Nos. 1, 3 & 4 Coys in front line at HOUPLINES. 9th Royal Scots Heavy shelling on our right. 9 Black Watch made a raid on German trenches. Battn. on right, sustains on left.	
	16/9/16		Quiet day. Unsuccessful raid was carried out by 5th Gordons on our front. They obtained 1 prisoner. Lieut M.	
	17/9/16		Wet day, quiet. Our artillery active at night. Lieut M.	
	18/9/16		Do. Germans raided Royal Scots on our right but were repulsed. Lieut M.	
	19/9/16		Do. Quiet except for occasional shelling & trench mortars. Lieut M.	
	20/9/16		Do. Lieut M.	
	21/9/16		Do. Lieut M.	
ERQUINGHEM	22/9/16		Battalion was relieved by "B" Battn. 8th Australian Brigade at 10.30 am. & marched to billets in ERQUINGHEM. Lieut M.	
	23/9/16		Shot list of Box Respirators at ARMENTIERES. Battn. Lieut M.	
	24/9/16		Church Parade. Brigadier Genl. Hamilton inspected Officers. Lieut M.	
ESTAIRES	25/9/16		Battalion left ERQUINGHEM and marched to billets in ESTAIRES. Lieut M.	
	26/9/16		Brigade inspected by Genl. Plumer, G.O.C. 2nd Army on route march on occasion of our leaving the 2nd Army. Lieut M.	
	27/9/16		Good day. Coy. drill & training, Physical exercise. Battn. Lieut M.	
	28/9/16		Do. Lieut M.	
	29/9/16		Do. Lieut M.	
CANDAS	30/9/16		Battn. left ESTAIRES, & entrained at MERVILLE at 5 p.m. arriving at CANDAS about 10 p.m. and were billeted there. Lieut M.	

1/10/16. Lt. Col. William W.M.
Comdg. 8th Bn. Seaforth Hrs.

661

Vol 13

21.S.
5 sheets

Confidential

CONFIDENTIAL
No 21/A
HIGHLAND
DIVISION

War Diary

1/4th Battn. of Seaforth Highrs.

from 1st October 1916

to 31st October 1916

(Volume 25)

Army Form C. 2118.

WAR DIARY
or
INTELLIGENCE SUMMARY
(Erase heading not required.)

Instructions regarding War Diaries and Intelligence Summaries are contained in F. S. Regs., Part II. and the Staff Manual respectively. Title Pages will be prepared in manuscript.

Place	Date	Hour	Summary of Events and Information	Remarks and references to Appendices
CANDAS	1/10/16		Battalion rested in billets for the day. Company trained route marches.	
	2/10/16		Company route marches & physical training.	
SARTON	3/10/16		Battalion left CANDAS & marched with Brigade to SARTON about 9 miles march & billeted there.	
BUS-LES-ARTOIS	4/10/16		Battalion marched to BUS-LES-ARTOIS about 6 miles and were billeted in huts.	
COURCELLES	5/10/16		Left BUS & marched last & went into bivouac near COURCELLES. 700 men went supplied for R.E. work from 8 pm to 2 am digging a new communication trench.	
	6/10/16		Cold wet day. 390 men supplied for R.E. work digging.	
	7/10/16		Wet day. 650 men supplied for carrying parties & digging.	
COLINCAMPS	8/10/16		Battalion moved to COLINCAMPS & went into bivouacs. 600 men on R.E. fatigue.	
	9/10/16		Cold day. 600 men on R.E. fatigue.	
	10/10/16		Good day. 650 men on fatigue carrying Trench Mortar Ammunition & digging.	
	11/10/16		650 men on usual fatigue. Battalion was relieved by 4th Londons & marched by Companies to LOUVENCOURT in billets.	
LOUVENCOURT	12/10/16		250 men supplied for fatigue.	
	13/10/16		Wet day. 20 men on coal fatigue. Battn. at baths, clearing up & resting. Attack practice at 2.30 pm. Draft of 20 Other ranks from 9th Bayonets arrived & posted 10 each to B. 2. 3. Companies.	
	14/10/16		Battn. Company Training & drill. Officers at Bayonet fighting under R.S.M.	
	15/10/16		Battn. Church Parade. Brigade Attack Scheme in afternoon. Net erection.	
	16/10/16		Battn. Coy. training & drill. Brigade Attack Scheme. Football match.	
RAINCHEVAL	17/10/16		Battalion moved to billets in RAINCHEVAL about 4 miles away.	

WAR DIARY or INTELLIGENCE SUMMARY

Army Form C. 2118.

(Erase heading not required.)

Place	Date	Hour	Summary of Events and Information	Remarks and references to Appendices
LEALVILLERS	18/10/16		Battalion marched to bivouacs near LEALVILLERS about 4 miles. Very wet & muddy.	
	19/10/16		Very wet & cold. Our guns active all day.	
	20/10/16		Bright day but cold. Boys at Physical training & Officers at Bayonet fighting. Attack practice in afternoon.	
	21/10/16		Bright cold day. Physical training etc.	
	22/10/16		Cold day. Battalion relieved 6th London in reserve, 2 Coys in village of AUCHONVILLERS H.Q. & remainder of Battalion in bivouacs in wood behind MAILLY MAILLET. Heavy bombardment by our guns all day.	
	23/10/16		Wet day. 450 Bun supplied for R.E. fatigue. Enemy shelled wood behind MAILLY-MAILLET. Our guns also active. Draft of 2 men arrived.	
	24/10/16		Wet day. 3/5 men on R.E. fatigue. Major R.S. Hunt who was attached to Battalion since July left to command 9th Royal Lancashire Regt. 2 Lt. Turnbull arrived from 5th Seaforths and posted to No. 1 Coy.	
	25/10/16		Wet day. 20 men supplied for R.E. fatigue.	
TRENCHES	26/10/16		Battalion relieved 6th Black Watch in firing line (S.W. of BEAUMONT HAMEL Q.15.b.25.15 - Q.17.a.44.66 Sheet 57d S.E. 1/20000) Nos. 1, 2 & 3 Coys in front line & No. 4 Coy in support, 9th Royal Scots on left and Royal Marines on right. Our own & enemy aeroplanes very active & a fight took place between a number of enemy planes & ours, two or three being taken down. Bombardment by our artillery in the evening & unsuccessfully raided by 6th Black Watch & 5th Gordons. Enemy artillery active during night. Repairing & clearing trenches.	
	27/10/16		Cold dull day. Our own & enemy artillery active.	
	28/10/16		Cold wet day. Enemy artillery again active, shells landing near Batt. H.Q. & communication trench. Our own 2" Stokes guns fired gas shells from N.2 to 3 from 9 again at night.	

Army Form C. 2118.

WAR DIARY
INTELLIGENCE SUMMARY
(Erase heading not required.)

Instructions regarding War Diaries and Intelligence Summaries are contained in F. S. Regs., Part II. and the Staff Manual respectively. Title Pages will be prepared in manuscript.

Place	Date	Hour	Summary of Events and Information	Remarks and references to Appendices
TRENCHES	28/10/16		Our heavy & field Artillery also shelled enemy trenches. Fifty 9.5" mortars of liquid gas were fired off 11 p.m. by R.E's on our front, the enemy sending up flares & replied with shrapnel & H.E. on our supports & communication trenches doing considerable damage. Work of repairing trenches continued.	
	29/10/16		Cold day. Enemy artillery & trench mortars active damaging our trenches in several places. Our guns were not so active as on previous days. Repairing & cleaning trenches carried out.	
	30/10/16		Very wet day. Enemy artillery again active especially on our trenches. Battalion was relieved by 4th Black Watch & marched by platoons to billets in LEALVILLERS. Casualties during last tour in trenches were 3 wounded.	
LEALVILLERS	31/10/16		Bright day. Cleaning up & resting.	

R A Lewsell
Capt
for Lt. Col.
Cmdg 4th Seaforth Hdrs.

Vol 14

Confidential

WAR DIARY

of

1/4th Batt. Seaforth Highlanders

from 1/11/16
to 30/11/16

(VOL 26)

WAR DIARY
or
INTELLIGENCE SUMMARY

(Erase heading not required.)

Army Form C. 2118.

Place	Date	Hour	Summary of Events and Information	Remarks and references to Appendices
LEALVILLERS	1/11/16		Bright day - Baths; 100 men on road cleaning	
"	2/11/16		" - 100 men cleaning roads, remainder Physical training	
"	3/11/16		" - Attack practice	
"	4/11/16		Baths; attack practice; 120 men went up to line in buses, working party digging and carrying. Capt. INCH 11/s Royal Scots joined Battn as 2nd in Command.	
"	5/11/16		Church parade. Battn moved to huts in MAILLY WOOD E	
MAILLY WOOD	6/11/16		Resting. Preparation to going into line	
"	7/11/16		Battn relieved 4th fordns in Right sector of line opposite BEAUMONT HAMEL;	
Trenches	8/11/16		Weather dull & heavy; much rain during night. Enemy shelled heavily during night and early morning, particularly ESSEX Trench, TIPERARY and THURLES Dumps. Trenches in awful condition, falling in and impassable nearly everywhere. Several dug-outs collapsed and a number of men were buried, two being killed.	
"	9/11/16		Battn H.Q. moved to advanced Battle H.Q. in FETHARD St. During night enemy shelled with tear-shell and gas.	
"	10/11/16		Enemy front line and BEAUMONT HAMEL heavily shelled by our artillery for 3½-4 an hour in the early morning, the whole of the Corps Artillery cooperating. No retaliation. Received orders that we would be relieved by 5th Seaforths, which were cancelled later.	

Army Form C. 2118.

WAR DIARY
or
INTELLIGENCE SUMMARY
(Erase heading not required.)

Instructions regarding War Diaries and Intelligence Summaries are contained in F. S. Regs., Part II. and the Staff Manual respectively. Title Pages will be prepared in manuscript.

Place	Date	Hour	Summary of Events and Information	Remarks and references to Appendices
Trenches	11/11/16		Our artillery again bombarded enemy trenches and BEAUMONT HAMEL from 5am - 6.15am. No enemy retaliation. Constant shelling by our artillery during day, also by trench mortars; gas was discharged from Q.5 mortars at "Y" Ravine. Received orders to be relieved by 4th Gordons – again cancelled.	
"	12/11/16		weather a little brighter. Our artillery again shells enemy lines and BEAUMONT HAMEL. Orders definitely received that tomorrow "Z" day; Zero hour 5.45am. Relieved in afternoon by units of 153rd Inf Bde, who took up their positions for attack next morning. Marched back to FORCEVILLE.	
FORCEVILLE	13/11/16	5.45am	After short preliminary intense bombardment 152nd + 153rd Bdes attacked and captured BEAUMONT HAMEL and established a line to the E. of BEAUMONT HAMEL. 63rd (Naval Division) on right and 2nd Division on our left. Numerous prisoners.	
MAILLY-WOOD E.	"	9.am	Commenced at FORCEVILLE and Battn moved up to huts in MAILLY WOOD. E. 15 minutes notice.	
MAILLY WOOD E.	14/11/16		Attack proceeding; BEUCOURT captured by 63rd Div.	
MAILLY WOOD E.	15/11/16		Still lying in MAILLY WOOD in constant readiness.	
" "	"	3pm	Moved up to line and relieved 7th A.F.S.H. - 2 companies in front line, NEW MUNICH trench and 2 Companies in support in prev. line. Bn H.Q. in	
Trenches			old German H.Q. at BEAUMONT HAMEL. Enemy shelling was heavily with 5.9in whilst relief proceeding; mostly falling in vicinity of Bn. H. Q. Casualties. 2nd Lt. CRICHTON killed; Lt. WATT wounded; 30 other ranks killed, 8 O.R. wounded; 2 missing	

WAR DIARY or INTELLIGENCE SUMMARY

Army Form C. 2118.

Place	Date	Hour	Summary of Events and Information	Remarks and references to Appendices
Trenches	16/11/16		Enemy shelled BEAUMONT HAMEL all day with 5.9. Considerable damage to MUNICH trench and the line. Casualties: 9 other ranks killed and 6 other ranks wounded, 11 other ranks.	Yes
"	17/11/16	5 p.m.	Two companies in front line relieved by 17th H.L.I. who were going to attack MUNICH trench on following morning. One company went back into dugouts in WAGON ROAD, the others came back to dugouts near Bn. H.Q. Enemy shelling very heavily during relief. 2nd Lt. M.M. MACKENZIE severely wounded. Casualties: 3 O.Rs. drowned, 8 O.Rs. wounded. 2nd Lt. KYNOCH showed out in no mans land to bring in a wounded Argyll did not return.	Yes
—	18/11/16	6 a.m.	17th H.L.I. attacked MUNICH trench, but held up by M.G. fire and suffered heavy casualties. Attack failed. Enemy again shelled BEAUMONT HAMEL strongly with 5.9. 2nd Lt. KYNOCH missing all day until 4 p.m. when he returned. Our casualties been 8 O.Rs. wounded, 16 O.Rs.	Yes 8 O.Rs wounded 16 O.Rs
—			2 Companies of 4th Gordons reinforced front line during afternoon. 17th H.L.I. relieved during early morning by a Batt. of Lancashire Fusiliers. The Batt. relieved by 6th Gordons at 10 hrs. and marched back to MAILLY WOOD.	Yes
"	19/11/16			Yes
MAILLY WOOD	20/11/16		Resting all day and cleaning up.	Yes
"	21/11/16		Fine day. Use of baths in MAILLY WOOD. Kit inspection.	Yes
"	22/11/16		A party of 2 ORs men cleaning up camp. Remainder resting. 2nd Lt. M.M. MACKENZIE reported to have died yesterday at CONTAY; a party went to CONTAY to his funeral.	Yes
"	23/11/16		Fine day. Batt. moved to VARENNES. Billeted in huts.	Yes
VARENNES	24/11/16		Batt. moved again to PUCHEVILLERS and took one camp from 96th Gordons.	Yes
PUCHEVILLERS	25/11/16		Bad weather. Men engaged cleaning up + improving camp.	Yes

Army Form C. 2118.

WAR DIARY
or
INTELLIGENCE SUMMARY
(Erase heading not required.)

Instructions regarding War Diaries and Intelligence Summaries are contained in F. S. Regs., Part II. and the Staff Manual respectively. Title Pages will be prepared in manuscript.

Place	Date	Hour	Summary of Events and Information	Remarks and references to Appendices
AVELUY	26/11/16		Brigade moved here today from PUCHEVILLERS. Batt billetes in huts near AVELUY	See
"	27/11/16		Very cold and windy. Working parties unloading trains	See
"	28/11/16		Still very cold. Working party 350 men unloading trains and work on RE dump near POZIERES. Improving camp.	See
"	29/11/16		Still cold. About 150 men working unloading trains. Continues improving camp; laying trench boards. Camp extremely muddy.	See
"	30/11/16		170 men unloading trains; work on roads. Weather still very cold.	See

30/11/16

J. Mulhaird Lt Col
Cmdg 9th 4/ Wafs. H. Fus.

4th Seaforth Highlanders.

War Diary

From 1.12.16
to
31.12.16

(Vol. 2".)

WAR DIARY
or
INTELLIGENCE SUMMARY.

(Erase heading not required.)

Army Form C. 2118.

Place	Date	Hour	Summary of Events and Information	Remarks and references to Appendices
Near Avelut	Dec 1st		The Bn. is ater in "Bruce" huts. Strong wind blowing – very cold. Working Party at AVELUY SIDING, loading trucks & repairing roads. Ground still hard with previous frost.	
	2nd		AVELUY shelled heavily – not much damage. Two men of the Battalion were killed, and one wounded. Working Party at AVELUY SIDING loading trucks etc. The same as yesterday.	
WOLFE HUTS	3rd		The Bn. moved to WOLFE HUTS in relief of the 9th Bn Gordon Hers. Still very cold weather. Party supplied to R.E's at 9.30 pm to dry trench mat front line.	
	4th		Very frosty & extremely cold. Carrying Parties supplied to R.E's during day, and also at night.	
	5th		Frost thaws – it commenced to rain very heavy. Gum Carrying Parties are supplied to R.E's. Ground very heavy & night very dark.	
	6th		The Bn. moved into the right sector of the Line. Gum Boots carried. Very wet under foot & very dark. Men exhausted. Relief of 4th Bn. Gordon Hers. (in front of COURCELETTE) completed.	

Army Form C. 2118.

WAR DIARY
or
INTELLIGENCE SUMMARY.
(Erase heading not required.)

Place	Date	Hour	Summary of Events and Information	Remarks and references to Appendices
	Dec			
TRENCHES	7th		Dull & miserable weather. Men in front line suffered hard to try to improve trenches. Condition extremely bad. No relief at all in time part of line. Impossible to get hot food. No shells in front line. Men miserable than yesterday. Very wet work. Still trying to improve trenches – very difficult to make headway. Lewis Guns relieved - proceeded to OVILLERS HUTS.	
	8th			
HUTS	9th		Heavy rain all day. Wet in Lewis Copeles. Parties (Offr & Enemy) out in "no man's land" bringing dead – flying Post Hqr. Nothing fired. Bn. relieved at night – proceeded to OVILLERS HUTS.	
	10th		Bn. moved to BOUZINCOURT – huts in farm. Weather wet and & cold.	
BOUZINCOURT	11th		Rain. The following were awarded the military medal for gallantry at BEAUMONT-HAMEL:—	
			Nos. 2039 Pte C.E. FILE	
			" 2222 " Thos. MELTON	
			" 1406 Cpl. ROBT. MOORE	
			" 4508 Pte DANL. HANDCOCK	
			" 3408 Pte M.A. MOORE	
			" 4303 " MIEL MCPHERSON	
			" 3060 " G. GARDINER	
			" 4144 " W. IRELAND (and 1st/4th T.M.B)	
	12th		(see next sheet)	

WAR DIARY or INTELLIGENCE SUMMARY

Army Form C. 2118.

Place	Date	Hour	Summary of Events and Information	Remarks and references to Appendices
BOUZINCOURT	Dec. 12th		Divs. Party sent out on drainage work. The C.O. presented cards to the NCO's & Men mentioned for gallantry at BEAUMONT-HAMEL. C.S.M. T. ROSS appointed in Commission & posted to No 2. Coy. WD	
	13th		Whole day – very cold. Baths at BOUZINCOURT opened to the Battalion. Same working party as yesterday. 2/Lt. J. SMITH joined the Battalion & posted to No 2. Coy. Bn. 1st Inspection. WD	
	14th		Very wet. Bn. remained in billets – cleaning clothing &c WD	
	15th		60 men working at AVELUY ADDS draining Truck. 100 men laying pipe line. 30 men working on same draining. 2/Lt Record joined Bn. posted to No 1 Coy	
	16th		Bn. moved to OVILLERS HUTS. Party of 50 men pushing trollys. WD	
OVILLERS HUTS	17th		Cold & frosty. Party of 100 working on overland tracks Church Parade in Pastors Church. Bent. WD	
	18th		Still cold & frosty. Party of 200 working on overland tracks. C.O. went on LEAVE. WD	
	19th		OVILLERS HUTS shelled evening & early morning – no casualties. 100 men swinging case – camp improved. Bn. Church held in Sentier Church tent. Draft of 69 arrived from Base. WD	

WAR DIARY
INTELLIGENCE SUMMARY
(Erase heading not required.)

Army Form C. 2118.

Place	Date	Hour	Summary of Events and Information	Remarks and references to Appendices
HUTS Villers	24th		Hand grenade. OVILLERS HUTS shelled again - no casualties. Party of 75 sending trollies. 250 men burying cable. Remainder from improve camp.	
	26th		Bn moved into line. 2 Coys into QUARRIES + 2 Coys into WOLFE HUTS. Duck boards inclined to rain.	
	25th		Very wet. Extremely muddy training.	
TRENCHES	23rd		Very windy. A number of men buried about the QUARRIES	
	24/2		2 Coys from WOLFE HUTS moved into front line in relief of the 1st Essex Regt. Very rockets sent up as a lot "S.O.S." Enemy quiet in front line during relief. Enemy Artillery	
	25/2		Thaw day. Damp, windy. Rather a nice day. Frost at fixed times all day.	
	26/2		Very wet. Nothing unusual happened during the tour.	
HUTS	27/2		Good day. Bn relieved and proceeded to OVILLERS HUTS men very worn out.	
	28th		Bn moved to BOUZINCOURT + arrangements same killed or before.	
	29th		Duck + wet. Bn - no fuel for fire. No 1, 2, 3+4 Coys allotted baths at	
BOUZINCOURT			General clearing up of clothing etc. Kit Inspection	

Army Form C. 2118.

WAR DIARY
or
INTELLIGENCE SUMMARY.

(Erase heading not required.)

Instructions regarding War Diaries and Intelligence Summaries are contained in F. S. Regs., Part II. and the Staff Manual respectively. Title pages will be prepared in manuscript.

Place	Date	Hour	Summary of Events and Information	Remarks and references to Appendices
BOUZINCOURT	Dec 30th		Companies inspected by C.O. Remainder of men allotted huts. Very damp. Brigade concert in Evening.	
	31st		Bath granted holiday, in second of men in new year's day. Band played in new year.	

Nd Evrell
Capt.
for O.C. 4th Seaforth Highlanders

Confidential

CONFIDENTIAL.
No 21 (H)
HIGHLAND DIVISION.

War Diary

of

1/4th Battn Seaforth Highlanders

Volume 28

from 1st January 1917
to   31st January 1917

Army Form C. 2118.

WAR DIARY
or
INTELLIGENCE SUMMARY
(Erase heading not required.)

Instructions regarding War Diaries and Intelligence Summaries are contained in F. S. Regs., Part II. and the Staff Manual respectively. Title Pages will be prepared in manuscript.

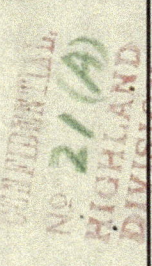

CONFIDENTIAL
No. 21 (A)
HIGHLAND DIVISION

Place	Date	Hour	Summary of Events and Information	Remarks and references to Appendices
In the field	Jan 1st		The Battalion moved up; part to WOLFE HUTS + part to dug-outs; from BOUZINCOURT. The Battalion commenced work, exclusively for R.E. Weather dull. Y.P.G.	
"	2.		Work was done under R.E. Weather dull. Y.P.G.	
"	3.		Work was done under R.E. - wiring etc., also in improvement of camp. Y.P.G. Weather - very wet.	
"	4.		Work was done under R.E. 5 men were wounded near POZIÈRES stamp. The Adjutant proceeded to Junior Officers' School, ALDERSHOT. Y.P.G. Weather - still very wet.	
"	5.		Work was done under R.E., - wiring etc. 6 men were gassed at night while wiring in front of COURCELETTE. In the early morning the huts occupied by the Battalion were shelled - no casualties. Weather clear; inclined to be frosty. Y.P.G.	
"	6.		Work was done under R.E. 2 Officers v 6 O.R.s proceeded to courses of instruction. 6 men were gassed. Weather - very damp + dull. Y.P.G.	

WAR DIARY or INTELLIGENCE SUMMARY

Army Form C. 2118.

Place	Date	Hour	Summary of Events and Information	Remarks and references to Appendices
In the field	Jan 7th		Divine Services were held. Weather - frosty with some sunshine.	
"	" 8 "		There were the usual working parties. Weather - wet.	
"	" 9 "		The usual working parties were cancelled owing to a three days' bombardment by heavy artillery commencing. Capt. HENDERSON returned from Senior Officers' School, ALDERSHOT. Weather - dull & very cold.	
"	10 "		Working parties for R.E. consisted of 42 men only in all. The R.S.M. proceeded on leave. Weather - dull & cold.	
"	11 "		Working parties for R.E. consisted of 75 men only in all. Weather - dull & cold.	
"	12 "		42 men were supplied for R.E. work. Weather dull & cold.	
"	13 "		H.Q., 10, 11 Coy, & Specialists marched from WOLFE HUTS at 2 p.m. & reached RUBEMPRÉ at 9 p.m. Battalion Transport leaving preceded them leaving the previous afternoon. Billets were occupied in RUBEMPRÉ after arrival.	

Army Form C. 2118.

WAR DIARY
or
INTELLIGENCE SUMMARY
(Erase heading not required.)

Instructions regarding War Diaries and Intelligence Summaries are contained in F.S. Regs., Part II. and the Staff Manual respectively. Title Pages will be prepared in manuscript.

Place	Date	Hour	Summary of Events and Information	Remarks and references to Appendices
On the field	Jan 14th		The Bn. were conveyed in motor buses from RUBEMPRÉ to BERNEUIL leaving at 9.30 a.m. & arriving at 2 p.m. On arrival went into billets.	J.H.
" "	" 15th		The Bn. marched from BERNEUIL at 10.30 a.m. & arrived at MILLENCOURT at 4 p.m. & were billeted there.	J.H.
" "	" 16th		The Bn. marched from MILLENCOURT at 9.45 a.m. & arrived at FAVIÈRES at 4.30 p.m. The remainder of the Battalion arrived with the Transport at ACHEUX on the night of the 15th & detrained having entrained at ABBEVILLE early in the morning of the 16th. This party was left behind to carry out work for the 2nd Division which relieved the 51st Division. The men of this party suffered considerably from cold & fatigue owing to defective arrangements for the journey. Left (acting) J.R. BLACK was in charge of this party & food & substance with him.	J.H.
" "	17th		The Bn. were issued with clothing, equipment, etc. Weather cold & wet with some snow but short of clothing.	J.H.
" "	18th		" " " " on 17th. Weather cold.	J.H.
" "	19th		" " " " & on 17th. Inspections under company arrangements.	J.H.
" "	20th		Inspection of Battalion by C.O. (acting - Major INCH.) Weather very cold.	J.H.
" "	21st		Church Parade. The C.O. returned from leave. Weather frosty.	L.F.
" "	22nd		Inspection of Battalion by conferring by G.O.C. 157th Inf. Bde. (Brig. Gen. HAMILTON.) Weather frosty	J.H.

WAR DIARY or INTELLIGENCE SUMMARY

Army Form C. 2118.

Place	Date	Hour	Summary of Events and Information	Remarks and references to Appendices
On the Field	Jan. 23rd		Company training. Capt. HENDERSON attached to 6th Black Watch, provisionally to form that unit. Weather - very frosty.	
"	24th		Route march & company training. Weather very frosty.	
"	25th		Company training & reorganization. Recreational training for Divisional Sports. Weather very frosty. Party about 140 men, led baths ran athe of clean under-clothing, at PONTHOILE (Ref. Map FRANCE, ABBEVILLE Sheet 14, 1/100,000). Weather very frosty.	Y.F.P.
"	26th		Company training. Recreational training for Divisional Sports. Weather very frosty.	Y.F.P.
"	27th		Company training. Recreational training for Divisional Sports. Weather very frosty.	Y.F.P.
"	28th		Church Parade. Recreational training for Divisional Sports. Weather very frosty.	Y.F.P.
"	29th		Company training. One company practised the attack in the open very frosty. 60 men were provided for work at ROMAINE station (Ref. Map FRANCE, ABBEVILLE, Sheet 14, 1/100,000). Weather - very frosty.	Y.F.P.
"	30th		Company training. Weather - very frosty.	Y.F.P.
"	31st		Inspection by G.O.C. Division (Major Gen. HARPER) of Battalion in attack practise from worked out trenches. Staff of Divisional Sports wore present. Special arrangements commenced. Weather - very frosty.	Y.F.P.

J. F. R. Maj. for
LIEUT. COLONEL
COMDG. 1/4th Bn. SEAFORTH HIGHRS.

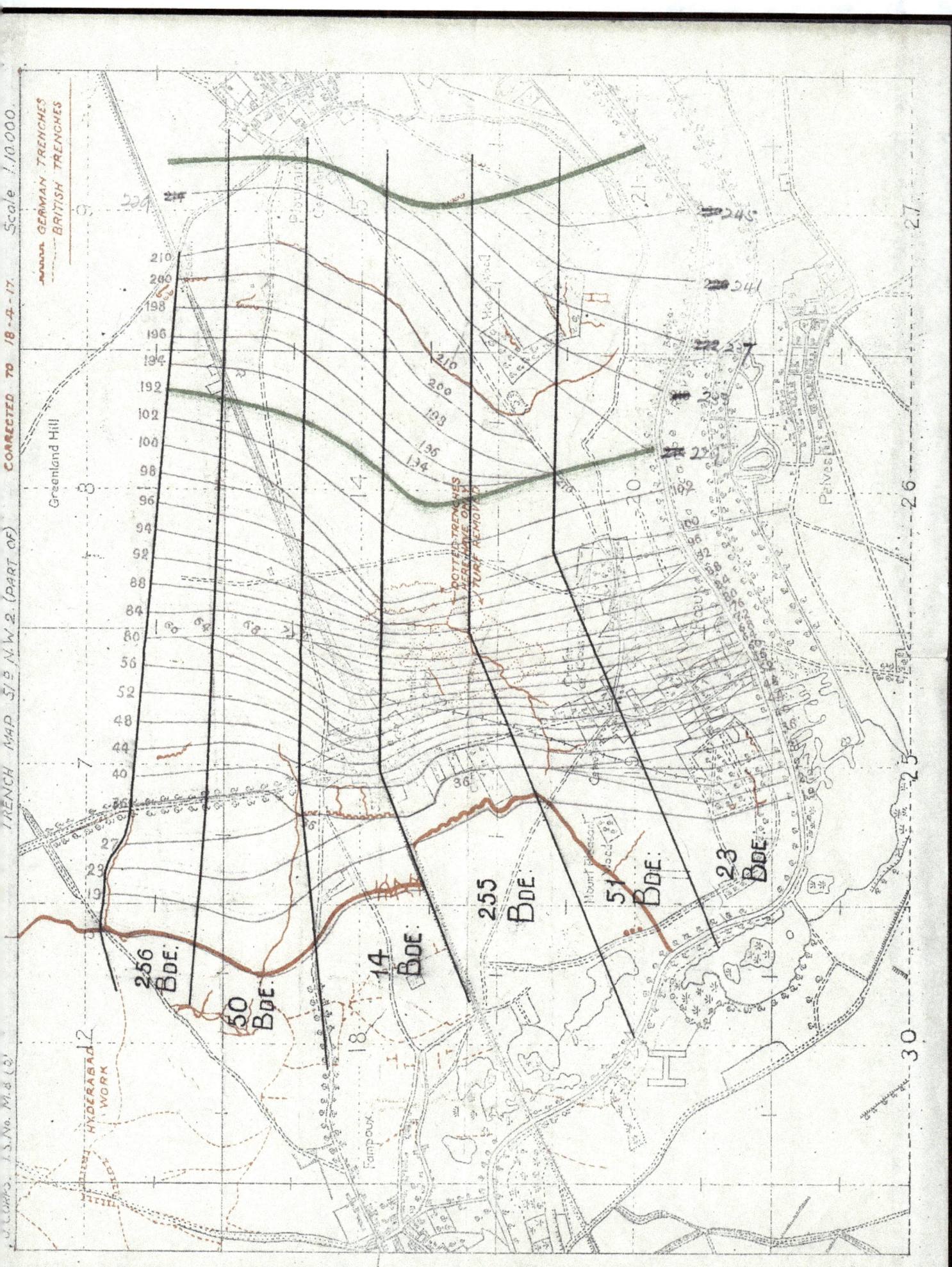

Vol 17

25-S.
5 sheets

Confidential

War Diary
of
1/4th Seaforth Highlanders
(Volume 29)

from   1st February 1917.
to   28th February 1917.

WAR DIARY or INTELLIGENCE SUMMARY

Army Form C. 2118

Place	Date	Hour	Summary of Events and Information	Remarks and references to Appendices
FAVIERES	1/2/17		Battalion at rest billets in FAVIERES. Weather very frosty. Companies carried out training and attack practice. Baths at PONTHOILE. The delayed New Year dinner for No 1 Coy took place at LE CROTOY and was a great success. A/h.	
	2/2/17		Companies carried out, Bayonet fighting, bombing & company training. No 4 Coy New Year dinner at LE CROTOY. A/h.	
	3/2/17		Bn. training. No.3 Coy New Years dinner at LE CROTOY. A/h.	
			Coy training. Church Parade. Major R. Trueloveleft to Staff appointment in 152nd Inf. Brigade. A/h. The Battalion, Coy training. The Battalion team won Brigade Bayonet Fighting Competition.	
FORREST L'ABBAYE	4/2/17		Very cold & slight snowfall. The Battalion left FAVIERES at 1 p.m. & marched to FORREST L'ABBAYE arriving at 3.30 p.m. & billeted there. A Draft of 88 other ranks joined the Battalion. A/h.	
FONTAINE SUR-MAYE	5/2/17		Very frosty. Battalion marched to FONTAINE-SUR-MAYE about 8 miles. The draft was inspected by the C.O. and posted to Companies. A/h.	
NOEUX	7/2/17		Battalion marched to NOEUX via AUX-LE-CHATEAUX & billeted there. Very cold & frosty. A/h.	
NUNCQ	8/2/17		Battalion marched to NUNCQ about 9 mile. Roads were very bad. Weather cold. A/h.	
MARQUAY	9/2/17		Battalion marched to MARQUAY about 9 miles & went into billets there. A/h.	
	10/2/17		Remained for the day at MARQUAY. Test inspection, running gas helmet drill. A/h.	
ECOIVRES	11/2/17		Battalion marched by main ARRAS road to huts near ECOIVRES arriving at 3.30 p.m. A/h.	
	12/2/17		Weather slightly warmer. 75 men supplied for work under R.E. one party at ACQ dump of tramp admitted out. A/h.	
	13/2/17		Very cold day. Two parties of 50 men supplied for work under R.E., one party at ACQ dump & one at R.E. yard MAROEUIL. Improvement & training of specialists under own Officers. A/h.	

WAR DIARY
or
INTELLIGENCE SUMMARY
(Erase heading not required.)

Army Form

Instructions regarding War Diaries and Intelligence Summaries are contained in F.S. Regs., Part II. and the Staff Manual respectively. Title Pages will be prepared in manuscript.

Place	Date	Hour	Summary of Events and Information	Remarks and references to Appendices
ECOIVRES	14/2/17		Weather frosty & cold. Following working parties supplied working under 12 E.a:- 100 min at R.E. yard MAROEUIL, 100 min at ACG dump, 114 min on permanent work at ST NICHOLAS and 30 min at ANZIN. Training of new Lewis Gunners & Bombers. M/Gr	
	15/2/17		Cold & frosty. Fatigue parties supplied as follows, 100 mm at ACG dump loading ammunition, 75 mm at MAROEUIL Station, 54 mm permanent party under R.E. at ST AUBIN. M/hr	
	16/2/17		Still frosty. At 5.20 a.m. a German aeroplane flew over ECOIVRES & dropped bombs killing two civilians. Following parties supplied. 75 mm at MAROEUIL Station, 50 mm at ACG dump, 50 mm at XVIIth Corps Ammunition park. M/hr	
	17/2/17		Dull & misty. A slight thaw. 100 min supplied for work at MAROEUIL 75 mm at ACG dump	
	18/2/17		Wet & misty & ground very muddy. Church service. 100 mm working at R.E. yard MAROEUIL	
	19/2/17		Dull day. Baths at ACG. allotted to Co. 100 mm on wk. at R.E. yard MAROEUIL. Training of Specialists under Instructors. 2 Lieuts HARVEY and ABEL joined Battalion from England. M/hr	
	20/2/17		Cold & wet. 100 min on R.E. work at MAROEUIL. Specialists continued training. M/hr	
BRAY WOOD	21/2/17		Dull day. 100 min on fatigue at MAROEUIL and 120 mm at ACG dump. Battalion moved to tents in BRAY WOOD about 1 mile away. Detached working parties rejoined Battalion. No 3 Coy billeted in ACG. M/hr	
TRENCHES ROCLINCOURT	22/2/17		24 Lewis Gunners under 2 Lt KYNOCH and 32 Bombers under 2 Lt D. ROSS went for training at CAVOURT. The Battalion relieved the 5th Seaforth Hrs in the front line at ROCLINCOURT on the same front as we occupied from March till July. Nos 3 & 4 Coys in the front line and Nos 1 & 2 Coys in support. The trenches were in a very bad condition and No. 3 Coy was unable to get up till early morning of 23rd. 9th Division were on our right and 2nd Canadian Division on our left. M/hr	

WAR DIARY or INTELLIGENCE SUMMARY

Army Form C. 2118

Place	Date	Hour	Summary of Events and Information	Remarks and references to Appendices
TRENCHES	23/2/17		Dull & cold. Cleaning & clearing trenches. Very little activity on either side. Two parties of 50 men working on trenches under R.E's. Enemy sent over a few trench mortars. M.W.	
	24/2/17		Day dull & cold & misty. Very quiet in the line. Usual parties under R.E's cleaning & repairing trenches. Patrols went out from Coys & were fired on after throwing bombs into enemy trenches. M.W.	
	25/2/17		Bright day. Our artillery was fairly active, cutting wire. 2 Lieuts. A.R. KYNOCH, D.L. TURNBULL, & H.F. SMITH left Battalion for England for transfer to M.G.C. R.S.M. Anolmon left Battalion to act as R.S.M. at Divisional Training Depot. Draft of 29 other ranks arrived at Transport. Cleaning & repairing trenches continued. M.W.	
	26/2/17		Dull day. Very little activity. One of our aeroplanes was hit & pursued by a German plane & brought down behind our lines. Major Inch went to hospital sick. M.W.	
MARDEUIL	27/2/17		Dull day. Enemy sent over a few trench mortars on our left. One of our aeroplanes was taken down. Battalion was relieved by 9th Royal Scots & went by companies to billets in MARDEUIL. We had only two casualties during tour in trenches. M.W.	
	28/2/17		Dull day. Parties of 3 Officers & 180 men supplied for work on trenches under 8th Royal Scots & 10 Officers & 60 men under R.E's working on Advanced Divisional H.Q. MARDEUIL. M.W.	

E. Mulhead Lt.Col.
Comdg. 4/ Seaforth H'rs.

1/3/17.

Confidential

War Diary

of

1/4th Battn. Seaforth Highlanders

from 1st March 1917   to   31st March 1917

(Volume 30)

WAR DIARY
or
INTELLIGENCE SUMMARY
(Erase heading not required.)

Army Form C. 2118.

Place	Date	Hour	Summary of Events and Information	Remarks and references to Appendices
MAROEUIL	1/3/17		In reserve in MAROEUIL. Bright day. Working parties of 180 men on trenches at ANZIN, 60 men on advanced from H.Q. supplied 2 Lt J.A. Mackenzie & 30 men sent to Divisional Training Battn. Training of new Lewis Gunners & Signallers. A/Intn	
	2/3/17		Bright day. Working parties as yesterday. Extra party of 1 Officer & 40 men supplied A/Intn	
	3/3/17		Bright day. Same working parties as yesterday. Training of Specialists. 2 Lts E.G. Munro & F.C. Slater joined Battalion from England. A/Intn	
	4/3/17		Frosty day. Same working parties as yesterday. Church Parade. A/Intn	
MAROEUIL WOOD	5/3/17		Cold day with snow fall. Same working parties as yesterday. Battalion moved to tents in MAROEUIL WOOD. A/Intn	
	6/3/17		Cold bright day. Working party of 8 Officers & 180 men on trench work from 7.30am to 3.30pm A/Intn Our aeroplanes & artillery active. Training of Specialists & training on wirecutting. A/Intn	
	7/3/17		Cold and windy. Same working party as yesterday. Training of Specialists. A/Intn	
	8/3/17		Cold and frosty. Same working party as yesterday. Training of Specialists. A/Intn	
	9/3/17		Working party of 9 Officers & 250 men supplied for trench work from 7.30 am to 3.30 pm. Major Grier returned from Hospital. A/Intn	
	10/3/17		Foggy and cold. Same working party as yesterday. A/Intn	
TRENCHES (SABLIERE)	11/3/17		Bright warm day. Battalion relieved 4th London in Sw off line Trenches. (SABLIERE). Relief complete by 6 pm. Trenches improved since last tour. Nos 3 & 4 Coys in front line, Nos 1 & 2 Coys in support. Col. Franks went to Hospital. A/Intn	
	12/3/17		Trenches falling in badly, impassable in places. All work undone. Working on all trenches night and day. Patrols went out to enemy wire. Enemy could be heard talking & coughing. A/Intn	
	13/3/17		Still wet. Trenches worse than ever. Bonval went sick in places. Working night & day in trenches but very little improvement to be seen. Clearing saps at night. 3 patrols sent out to enemy wire. No enemy encountered. Enemy attempted trench raid on Canadians but failed. A/Intn	

Army Form C. 2118.

WAR DIARY or INTELLIGENCE SUMMARY

(Erase heading not required.)

Instructions regarding War Diaries and Intelligence Summaries are contained in F. S. Regs., Part II. and the Staff Manual respectively. Title Pages will be prepared in manuscript.

Place	Date	Hour	Summary of Events and Information	Remarks and references to Appendices
TRENCHES (SABLIERE)	13/3/17		Enemy artillery activity increasing. Enemy aeroplanes very active over our lines. Enemy attempted to raid Brigade on our right. MNN.	
	14/3/17		Weather bitter. Trenches improving steadily. Nos. 1 & 2 Coys relieved Nos. 3 & 4 Coys in front line. Enemy very active with Artillery & Machine Guns. Enemy working parties observed. Wind dangerous. Expected attack by enemy but did not come off. MNN.	
	15/3/17		Weather very changeable. Condition of trenches steadily improving. Enemy artillery active in retaliation for 2" Trench Mortar fire. Avenue G badly blown in. Usual working parties on trenches. MNN.	
	16/3/17		Bright day. Avenue G cleared. Condition of trenches much improved. Aircraft of both sides active over lines. Arrival our fights. Battalion relieved by 1/6th Black Watch. Relief complete by 7.30 pm. Battn. H.Q. and Nos. 2, 3 & 4 Coys moved to ECURIE & No. 1 Coy to ANZIN in relief of 9th & 9.14th Battn. under 153rd Brigade for Nos. 1, 2, 3 & 4. Battn. under 154 Brigade for work. MNN.	
ECURIE	17/3/17		Weather very good. Several small working parties with R.E.'s on dumps. All available men working on assembly trenches in front of BONNAL. 7pm to 3 am. MNN.	
	18/3/17		Bright day. Work the as yesterday. Much progress made in cleaning assembly trenches. Much fight 1st and 2nd (Lt.Col Jekyll to Lt.Col Mn. Sept arrived also 3 Officers 2nd Lts J.A.R.G. Davidson, K. Russell & 9 H.S.G. Good day. Reinforcements of 65 men arrived at 8pm. Assembly trenches falling in & much work undone. MNN.	
	19/3/17		Very wet night.	
	20/3/17		Wet and cold. Capt. A.K. Train rejoined from Hospital. Usual working parties. MNN.	
	21/3/17		Showery & cold. Usual working parties. MNN.	
	22/3/17		Good day. Working parties same as yesterday. MNN.	
HUTS IN MAROEUIL WOOD	23/3/17		Bright warm day. Battalion relieved by 9th Royal Scots. Relief complete by 5.30pm. Moved to huts in MAROEUIL WOOD, arriving at 8pm. 4 casualties on way out from ECURIE. MNN.	

WAR DIARY or INTELLIGENCE SUMMARY

Army Form C. 2118.

Place	Date	Hour	Summary of Events and Information	Remarks and references to Appendices
HUTS IN MAROEUIL WOOD	24/3/17		Working party of 2 Officers and 100 men working at ANZIN under R.E.s from 7.30am to 3pm. Kit inspection. Cleaning clothing & equipment. P.M.M.	
	25/3/17		Good day. Usual working party working at ANZIN. 1 Officer & 50 men laying out practice trenches. Organised for attack and inspection. Attack practice under Coy arrangements. Very wet. Usual working parties. Battalion practice.	
	26/3/17		Gymnir on range practice. Attack scheme explained to Officers by C.O. Lewis Gun. Waddell joined Battalion from England. 2 Lts. R.E. Spinks-Ross and T.B. P.M.M.	
	27/3/17		Rain & snow in afternoon. All available specialists under training in forenoon. Usual party of 1 Officer & 100 men to Anzin. Baths at ACQ from 9am to 1pm for H.Q. & Nos. 2 & 4 Coys. Attack practice by Battalion in afternoon. P.M.M.	
	28/3/17		Dull showery day. Usual working party at Anzin. All specialists under training in forenoon. Attack practice in afternoon. Football matches in evening. Officers v. N.C.Os. resulted in a win for N.C.Os. by 3-2. Unloading party at MAROEUIL Station of 1 Officer & 50 men worked from 7pm to 5.30am. P.M.M.	
	29/3/17		Very wet. Battalion in position for practice attack on BLACK LINE. Zero time 11am. Brigadier General Hamilton was present & discussed scheme with Officers after practice. P.M.M.	
	30/3/17		Very wet & cold. Companies & Specialists training in forenoon. Evacuation in afternoon. Football match between Battalion team & 4th D.A.C. ended in a draw of 2 goals each.	
	31/3/17		Stormy & cold. Vicinity of camp shelled repeatedly but no casualties. 2 Lt. Gunn-Ross went to Hospital. 2 Lt. J.B. Mackenzie & 23 men returned from Divisional Depot Battalion. P.M.M.	

J.W. Mulhearn Lt Col
Comg 9th (Scottish) H.L.I.

31/3/17

(Confidential)

War Diary

of

1/4th Battn. Seaforth Highlanders

(Volume 31)

from   1st April 1917

to   30th April 1917.

Army Form C. 2118.

WAR DIARY
or
~~INTELLIGENCE SUMMARY.~~
(Erase heading not required.)

Instructions regarding War Diaries and Intelligence Summaries are contained in F. S. Regs., Part II. and the Staff Manual respectively. Title pages will be prepared in manuscript.

Place	Date	Hour	Summary of Events and Information	Remarks and references to Appendices
MAROEUIL WOOD	April 1		Showery day – Church parades in forenoon – Foot inspection – Battalion attack practice in afternoon. Lecture to officers. – 1 O. Rank wounded in MAROEUIL.	yes.
"	2		Cold & windy. Coy Companies at Bombing Practice. Qm. Stores moved to MAROEUIL & transport to BRAY. Heavy artillery active.	yes.
"	3		Battn. relieved 19th Royal Scots. ECURIE. H.Q. No 1 & 2 & 3 Coy in ECURIE. No 4 in ANZIN. Relief complete by 6.0 p.m. – Good weather.	yes.
ECURIE	4		Dull day. Our artillery active. Work carried on clearing out assembly Trenches in front line	
"	5		Bright day. Aeroplanes and artillery very active. Our guns bombarded enemy front system. Continuously. Cleaning & repairing Nissen Huts, continued. Captn. T.H. PEVERELL, Adjt. rejoined from Senior Officers Course, ALDERSHOT. Co. attended conference at Bde. H.Q.	yes.
"	6		Dull day. – Our artillery continually bombarded enemy trenches.	yes.
"	7		Bright day. H.Q. No. 1 and 3 Coys moved up to front line. Enemy shelled C.T. very heavily. Kearl(?) was slain in marching place. H.Q. in Ave. 2. A patrol was sent out from No 1, but recovered no round land – 1 man missing – Our artillery bombarded enemy trenches all day.	yes.
front line	8		Bright day – Enemy shelled our trenches with heavies. – No. 2 & 4 Coys moved from ECURIE to assembly position in front line.	yes.
A.7.C.7.2.3 4.23.0.4.6 slip 51.3 Nm.d Known			Attack	

Army Form C. 2118.

Instructions regarding War Diaries and Intelligence Summaries are contained in F. S. Regs., Part II. and the Staff Manual respectively. Title pages will be prepared in manuscript.

WAR DIARY
or
INTELLIGENCE SUMMARY.
(Erase heading not required.)

Place	Date	Hour	Summary of Events and Information	Remarks and references to Appendices
Front line (see previous page)	9	9.15am	Attack on Vimy Ridge. - The Battalion was ordered to attack and capture the German trenches from A.23.b.6. to A.23.b.0.5 and part of the LILLE ROAD salient to form a defensive flank between A.23.b.1.4.4 and A.23.a.2.6. This latter formed a separate operation but was carried out simultaneously with the remainder of the attack and closed into the Canadians on the left. The operation will be described separately. (Ref. map Sheet 51.B.N.W.1. 1/10000) The Battalion formed up in Assembly trenches in Busses. Leading wave 3 Platoons No.1 Company - 2nd wave 1st Platoon No. 2 and 4 Companies - 3rd wave 4 Platoons No. 2 & 4 Companies. On our right 10th Royal Scots. - At zero (4.45am) the whole moved off. The leading wave capturing the front line without opposition. - The 2 waves passed through front line and advanced against the enemy and were met by hot fire from machine guns and rifles through the barrage. The officers of No. 4 Coy. all became casualties and the advance stopped. Coys went then ald [added?] lie Company (No. 1) forward. The 2nd portion up. Efforts to piece and reposition such as [unclear] The situation was redressed by No. 1 Coy. advanced the objective reached and has been holding up the advance were put out of action by snipers. A mixed	

WAR DIARY
~~INTELLIGENCE SUMMARY~~

(Erase heading not required.)

Army Form C. 2118.

Place	Date	Hour	Summary of Events and Information	Remarks and references to Appendices
	9 (cont.)		A mixed party of all 3 Companies then proceeded to push forward up a trench to and of which touch was to be established with the Canadians on left, opposition being encountered all the way. The bombs here came into action also at this time.	See pp.
		7.15am	Junction with the CANADIANS.	
		2.15am	Report received from Companies containing disposition and casualties. O.C. will have them withdrawn his Company & Reman IX lines and Consolidate of captured position then proceeding. Sepan's operation on left. No. 3 Company & PEDLOW No. 1. Trenches in line. A party of Bombers and 1 Lewis gun emerged from a Tunnel with exit just to right of VILLE ROAD. A 2nd party engaged firm exit also. 30 yds to top of this. The Platoon on left and Bombing parties from Tunnel Co-workers no opposition and were not once entrained to Tunnel. The commander of party was severely wounded but heard firing occurred in the C.T.S. Two platoons advances for the purpose were insufficient and the remaining 2 Platoons were sent forward to the support from about 30 Germans were collected in an area which consists of the Railway Rails and Penult.	See

WAR DIARY
INTELLIGENCE SUMMARY
(Erase heading not required.)

Army Form C. 2118.

Place	Date	Hour	Summary of Events and Information	Remarks and references to Appendices
	9	am 8.15	fought hard till the Canadians worked round their rear. Two officers and 11 men were killed at this point. The Company were then withdrawn to the tunnel. Coy HQ was in communication with Brigade throughout. Lt. SCOTT offer a Post of the Bath Post reported to Dr HQ later about 30 Casualties carried in past line by evening 5.9". We took 167 prisoners 2 M.G.s and Six Trench Mortars. Casualties Killed. 7/Lts E.V.D. LESLIE, H.S.E. FOX, T.B. WADDELL, H.E.O. MURRAY, DIXON, A.J. DAVIDSON. 59 other ranks. Wounded 2/Lt D.E.F. MACGREGOR, R.J.E. ROSS, R.J. MACDONALD, D. BRANT. 151 other ranks. Missing 7 other ranks.	yes yes yes yes
	10		Wet day and cold. Nos 1 and 3 Coys in dug outs in German line — No 2 and 4 Coys were sent up forward in support to 4 Gordon Hldrs. Enemy artillery inactive. Nos 2 and 4 Coy relieved in evening by 15/3 Rl Scots and moved back to old German front line.	yes
	11		C.O. & Sgrs Collecting salvage. Bsth relieved by 2 H.L.I. and 17th Royal Fusiliers and marches to billets at LARASSET.	yes
LARASSET	12		Cleaning up clothing & equipment. Baths at FREVIN CAPELLE	yes
	13		Baths, drafts of 32 other ranks received	yes

Army Form C. 2118.

WAR DIARY
or
INTELLIGENCE SUMMARY

(Erase heading not required.)

Instructions regarding War Diaries and Intelligence Summaries are contained in F. S. Regs., Part II. and the Staff Manual respectively. Title Pages will be prepared in manuscript.

Place	Date	Hour	Summary of Events and Information	Remarks and references to Appendices
LHARASSET	14		Bath inspected by C.O.	
"	15		Very wet. — Battn marched to ST. LAURENT — BLANGY and relieved a Battn of 9th Divn in reserve	
St LAURENT BLANGY	16		Bad day. — Improving dug outs & cellars. — Providing S.A.A. SLR.s 2/Lt SLATER wounded	
"	17		Working parties supplied repairing roads	
"	18		Wet. — working parties mending roads	
"	19		Fine day. — working parties repairing roads — Draft of 140 other ranks arrived	
"	20		Fine. — Artillery trench & our side active	
"	21		Fine. Artillery active, having preparation for attack to take place 23rd	
"	22		Fine. Batt moved at night to position of assembly, in railway cutting near FAMPOUX. Attack to take place tomorrow. Bn in Bde Reserve.	
FAMPOUX	23	4.45	Attack on ROEUX and CHEMICAL WORKS. 9th Royal Scots, 7th A&SH, 1/4 Gordon Highlanders attack; we are in reserve.	
		8 a.m.	Received verbal orders from Brigadier to move with 2 companies up in support of 9th Royal Scots and take over command of the left sector of the Brigade front	

WAR DIARY or INTELLIGENCE SUMMARY

Army Form C. 2118

Place	Date	Hour	Summary of Events and Information	Remarks and references to Appendices
	23	am	Lt Col. McCLINTOCK who was wounded.	yes
		8.15	Numbers of platoons advanced SCARPE by small wooden bridge to right of Railway thour'gh an extremely heavy barrage of S.9.	yes
		8.55	Companies start to arrive — I was informed by Col. McClintock that his right brigade on our that his left attack had been completely demolished by our H.E. at junction of Railway (ARRAS - DOUAI Railway) and German front line and that a party of about 50 Germans were this morn' established at this point and still holding out. Lieut ANDERSON 14th [Royal Scots?] pointed out the exact spot and I proceeded to make arrangements to deal with this situation but delayed the matter on seeing a tank arriving. In order to get the tank to assist.	yes
		9.40	Tank reported village of ROEUX surrounded by us on both sides but Germans resisting in centre. I called a halt for assistance in attacking strong point mentioned. Waited for tank.	yes
		9.56	Tank bogged so proceeded as previously arranged.	yes
		11.15	Reported capture of point. About 20 of the enemy were killed – 30 prisoners taken. We suffered no casualties. This strong point had held up the 11th Gordons + 9th Royal Scots in initial advance. No M.G. reported firing from this	yes

WAR DIARY
or
INTELLIGENCE SUMMARY
(Erase heading not required.)

Army Form C. 2118

Place	Date	Hour	Summary of Events and Information	Remarks and references to Appendices
	23	am	was found + must have been previously withdrawn. The Germans are with egg bombs entrenched the 4th garden's Bankers who has hills [Renassas] apparently how no rifle grenades.	[yes]
		11.5	Ordered 2 Coys up to relieve forward posts line and to push on from there into CHEMICAL WORKS. 1 Coy in support, 1 in reserve. Lt-Capt Pedrow Right Coy advanced without opposition and establishes themselves in line of shell holes on E. of CHEMICAL works. Advance on W. of CHATEAU impossible owing to M.G. fire from Cemetery. Formed a defensive flank along Railway.	[yes]
			1.30 pg. (?) A disorganised turn out party of 153 Rd. were on our left holding a trench dug in rear.	[yes]
		pm 5.25	Ordered for intense bombardment of ROEUX & N. end of Cemetery as enemy concentration reported.	[yes]
		5.30	Enemy Counter attack from GREENLAND HILL cut up by rifle + M.Gun fire. The enemy attack developing from Roeux was shattered by artillery fire + the remnants dispersed by rifle M.G.un fire.	[yes]
		8.20	Reported Germans advancing and sent up 2 platoons to reinforce	[yes]

Army Form C. 2118.

WAR DIARY or INTELLIGENCE SUMMARY

(Erase heading not required.)

Place	Date	Hour	Summary of Events and Information	Remarks and references to Appendices
	23	Pm		
		8.45	Put up the S.O.S.	*[initials]*
		9	The advanced Company & Platoon retired to old German front line. The works of the CHEMICAL works had been shelled for some time by our own as well as the German artillery, & the forward platoon has suffered 15 casualties & been forced to retire. The 153 Bde had previously retired on the left. The Coy. & Platoon in advance had also suffered many casualties & the Coy Commander had been wounded. — The enemy were working round both flanks, ammunition had run out, supplies on the way up could not get there + as the enemy had worked round right flank, the Coy reluctantly withdrew. — The night passed quietly. — The enemy established 2 M. guns on line of road from Station — Chateau + about 50 [yards] occupied a house on S. of Rly and another 50 to Chateau. Patrols pushed out during night + were unable to advance more than 50" when fired on by M.G.s.	*[initials]*
	24	am		
		4.30	Enemy opened intense bombardment on CHEMICAL works	*[initials]*
		4.45	Enemy in considerable force seen advancing on CHEMICAL works from	*[initials]*

WAR DIARY
or
INTELLIGENCE SUMMARY

(Erase heading not required.)

Army Form C. 2118.

Place	Date	Hour	Summary of Events and Information	Remarks and references to Appendices
	24	a.m.	Hill cont. at 5 a.m. considerable enemy movement seen in villages. Enemy rifle & machine guns accounted for a good number.	fee
		5.0	All S.O.S rockets sent up. – Sent for artillery support by Rover bright and lamp. Enemy advance notwithstanding their own bombardment, but was stemmed.	fee
		6.0	All quiet by this time	fee
			The remainder of the day quiet except for our snipers.	fee
			Casualties Killed. Officers 2/Lt J HARVEY other ranks 15	
			Wounded. Capt A.K. FRASER, Lt. T.F. SCOTT, 2/Lt A. MACAULAY. Other ranks 60	fee
			Missing other ranks 5.	
			Relieved by 11th Suffolks + marched to billets in ARRAS.	fee
ARRAS	25		Entrained at ARRAS. – Detrained at LIGNY – ST FLOCHEL and marched to billets in MAISIERES. arriving 11pm	fee
MAISIERES	26		Cleaning up	fee

WAR DIARY or INTELLIGENCE SUMMARY

Army Form C. 2118.

Place	Date	Hour	Summary of Events and Information	Remarks and references to Appendices
	27		Baths - cleaning equipment etc. Draft of 88 other ranks arrived	See
	28		Good weather. Coy training & training of specialists.	See
	29		Fine. Church parade. 10 officers arrived. 2/Lts. ROBSON, J. DAVIDSON, W.N. COLLINS, W.S. DAVE, A. BRODIE, J.N. MACDONALD, J. BAIN, M. MURRAY. — 2/Lts. D.B.M. JACKSON and R.C. SPENCE — Ross rejoins from Hospital	See
	30		Bright weather. Coy training (open warfare) & training of specialists.	See

J.L. Mulvenie, Lt.Col.
Comdg. 8th W. Staffs la Btn.

Vol 20

(Confidential)

War Diary of
1/4th Battalion Seaforth Highlanders
(Volume 32)

from   1st May 1917.
  to   31st May 1917.

Army Form C. 2118.

WAR DIARY
or
INTELLIGENCE SUMMARY.
(Erase heading not required.)

Instructions regarding War Diaries and Intelligence Summaries are contained in F. S. Regs., Part II. and the Staff Manual respectively. Title pages will be prepared in manuscript.

Place	Date	Hour	Summary of Events and Information	Remarks and references to Appendices
MASIERES	1917 May 1		Six test drills. Company training & training of specialist. Very warm weather.	etc
"	2		Warm weather. Company training. G.O.C. Division came over in the afternoon for tea and to listen to Band. Rovings scouts and other sports held. Twelve military medals awarded for operations at Vimy Ridge on 9th April.	etc
"	3		Warm weather. Usual parades & training. Following officers arrived:- 2/Lts. T.V. Staub, J.T. Jenkins, C.R. Simpson, & Robson, posted to No.1 Coy. A.A. Pitcairn, Pr. Ballantyne, Collins, Davidson to No. 2 Coy. " H.A. MacIver, Macdonald, A. Brodie to No. 3 Coy. " M. Murray, W.S. Dane, J.A. Hermon, Bain, to No. 4 Coy. 2/Lts. D.M.B. Jackson and Spence. Ross returned from Hospital. Draft of 57 other ranks joined. — Co. went on leave. Concert in evening at which Balmoral (Bat. Concert ptrs) assisted.	etc
"	4		Usual parades. 2/Lt. G.M. Cooper returned from C.S. course.	etc
"	5		Good weather. Pte Robson to Hospital. Parades and training in the morning. Highland games in the afternoon which was very successful. Tea served on the ground. Lt Col. The Hon. I.M. Campbell and Local Scout piloted the prize.	etc
"	6		Sunday. Church parade. Bath. Band of 8th East. Lanc. played in the afternoon.	etc

WAR DIARY
or
INTELLIGENCE SUMMARY.

Army Form C. 2118.

Place	Date	Hour	Summary of Events and Information	Remarks and references to Appendices
MAISIERES	May 7		Very warm weather. 2nd Lt. G.M. Cooper went on L.S. Course to ETAPLES. Attack practice in morning. G.O.C. Division present. Sports in the afternoon.	yes
"	8.		Showers. Company training.	yes
"	9.		Warm day. Usual training. Lectured on P.T. & R.F. by Officer from 3rd Army M.G.	yes
"	10		Warm day. Usual training. Sports in afternoon, competition reinstated. Capt. BLACK went to Course at 3rd Army School	yes
"	11		will 7th A.I. & H Bdes. Coys. of 2 arms.	yes
"	12		Very warm. Company training in morning. Cricket in afternoon. Batt. marched from MAISIERES to Y. Hut near ETRUN ARRAS - ST. POL Road.	yes
			Via PERIN, HERMAVILLE Beauf, L.T.	yes
Y. HUT ETRUN	13		Church parade. Very warm	yes
"	14		Very warm. Moved into hills in ARRAS - H.Q. Rue de JERUSALEM. Batt - billeted in HOSPICE de VIELLARDS. Transport ST. NICHOLAS	yes
ARRAS	15		Dull day. Musketry practice. C.O. attended pare leave.	yes
"	16		Enemy shelled ARRAS during night 15/16th. Heavy German counterattack early morning of 16th against 152 Bde.	yes
		5am	Repulsed enemy blowing CHEMICAL works & ROEUX, Battn ordered to move up at once to ARRAS - LENS Railway embankment North of River SCARPE.	yes

Army Form C. 2118.

WAR DIARY
or
INTELLIGENCE SUMMARY.
(Erase heading not required.)

Place	Date	Hour	Summary of Events and Information	Remarks and references to Appendices
	16	8:30 a.m.	Moved up by platoons to Railway Embankment.	
	"	2 pm	Nos 2 & 4 Companies moved up to Railway Cutting S. of. FAMPOUX. Throughout the day the 152 Bde had repaired all the ground lost.	See
		7.30 pm	No 2 & 4 Companies advanced to COLOMBO trench E. of ROEUX in relief of 8th A.&S.H. - No. 4 Coy in COLOMBO trench, No. 2 Coy in CORONA trench N.E. of ROEUX and occupying posts in ROEUX.	See
		11 pm	H.Q. and Nos 1 & 3 Companies moved up in support. No. 3 Company into ROEUX wood; No 1 Coy into CUSP trench W. of ROEUX. H.Q. in CRUMP trench along the Sunken road W. of ROEUX & COTE trench works to E. of River SCARPE. On our left - 6th Black Watch; a our right river SCARPE with 29th Division on the other side of SCARPE. It rained heavily at night and ground became very muddy. The night was pitch dark. By this time the shelling had subsided.	See
			For the footnotes from 5th Bn. Seaforth Highlanders.	See
Front line E. of ROEUX	17th		All day. Our trench shelled at intervals. Many fellows wounded who had been lying in shell holes for some days. Were brought in. Building new posts; improving, repairing & consolidating position.	See

WAR DIARY
or
INTELLIGENCE SUMMARY.
(Erase heading not required.)

Army Form C. 2118.

Place	Date	Hour	Summary of Events and Information	Remarks and references to Appendices
Front line E. of ROEUX	18th		Bright day. Aeroplane activity on both sides. Enemy planes flying very low. Artillery of both sides active.	yes
"	"		No. 1 Coy relieved No. 4 in front line.	yes
"	19th		Bright day. Enemy shelling our tanks intermittently all day, particularly ROEUX and ROEUX wood. Working/consolidating position. Division on right attacked at night. Heavy enemy barrage on their front. Enemy aeroplane brought down by Lewis gun fire.	yes
"	20.		Bright day. Heavy bombardment on our right at day break. Relieved at night by 4th Gordon Hdrs and proceeded to Divisional Reserve at Railway Embankment (ARRAS-LENS Line) (V.O) SCARPE, W.O) ATHIES. (H.13.d. Ref. map. 51.B.N.W.). Casualties. Killed 2 oth. ranks; Died of wounds 1 oth. rank; Wounded 26 oth. ranks. Missing 2 oth. ranks.	yes
Railway Embankment H.13.d. Ref. Map 51.B.N.W.	21		Bright day. Cleaning up. Baths. Capt. HARRIS + 2/Lt Lt.C.B. HANNA went on leave.	yes
"	22.		Bright day. Improving dug outs + shelters. Kit inspection.	yes
"	23		" Bathing - Resting	yes
"	24		" "	yes
"	25		Warm Day. Attack practice. Battn went to Divisional Rest.	yes

WAR DIARY
or
INTELLIGENCE SUMMARY

(Erase heading not required.)

Army Form C. 2118.

Place	Date	Hour	Summary of Events and Information	Remarks and references to Appendices
	26		Warm day. Usual training.	
	27		" " "	
	28		" " Battn relieved 7th A. I.B.A. in support. Nos. 2 r 3 Coys in Sunken Road W.b) ROEUX + E. of SCARPE; — H.Q. I 1st Coy E. in Rail way Cutting S. of FAMPOUX. — 7th COYS found Battn and took over signal section.	See See
Support line W. of ROEUX	29.		Good day — Improving dug outs. Working Road side, See Digging C.T.S. & improving tracks. 20ther ranks awarded Dan to M.M. and 16 awarded M.M. for operation on 23rd April.	See
"	30		Heavy thunderstorm. Working improving tracks and a C.T.S. — Carrying R.E. stors to fon line. Casualties: 1 Other rank killed 5 Other ranks wounded. (a) Barts M.M. and (b) M.M. referred to List b) N.C.Os. men awarded.	See
			On 29th. (A) 200615 Sgt Sydney Lane 20082; L Sgt G Gardner. (b) 200986 Sgt G. Dawkenby 200251 Sgt M. Mackenzie 200056 Bte W 200148 Pte W Yule. 201256 Pte W Carmichael 200257 Pte a Mackenzie 201471, Murdoch 201294 L Sgt Mackenzie 200277 Pte A. Bates.	See
"	31		Relieved by 5th Camn Hrs (9th Division) and entrained train to billets in ARRAS.	See

G. Mcllwraith Lt.Col.

Confidential

War Diary
of
1/4th Battn Seaforth Highrs

Volume 33

from   1st June 1917.
to   30th June 1917.

Army Form C. 2118.

WAR DIARY
or
INTELLIGENCE SUMMARY.
(Erase heading not required.)

Instructions regarding War Diaries and Intelligence Summaries are contained in F. S. Regs., Part II. and the Staff Manual respectively. Title pages will be prepared in manuscript.

Place	Date	Hour	Summary of Events and Information	Remarks and references to Appendices
ARRAS	1/6/17		Battalion in billets at ARRAS. The Battalion entrained at No 2 Station ARRAS at 2 pm & arrived at TINQUES at 5.30 pm & marched to BAILLEUL - aus - CORNEVIL & went into billets there	yes
BAILLEUL	2/6/17		Warm day. Resting & cleaning up. A Draft of 3 Officers & 160 other ranks arrived from Depot Battalion. Officers were 2 Lts. L.A. HARRIS, ESST & GAINER & A. MUNRO.	yes yes yes
	3/6/17		SUNDAY. Church Service.	
VALHUON	4/6/17		Battalion marched off at 6.10 am & arrived at VALHUON at 8.30 am & billeted there	yes
LISBOURG	5/6/17		Battalion marched off at 8.30 am via BOYAVAL & HEUCHIN & arrived at LISBOURG at 1.30 pm. The day was very warm & marching very trying	yes
	6/6/17		Warm day. Short Battn. route march. boys bathing	yes yes
	7/6/17		The Battalion left LISBOURG in buses at 8 am. & went via ST. OMER to billets in LA PANNE near NORDAUSQUES arriving at 4 pm.	yes yes
LA PANNE	8/6/17		Showery day. Training of Companies & Specialists	yes yes
	9/6/17		do	yes yes
	10/6/17		Boys training at Attack practise. A Draft of 47 other ranks arrived.	yes
	11/6/17		Wet day. Attack practise. A draft of 12 details from Base arrived	yes
	12/6/17		Fine day. Brigade Attack practise.	yes
	13/6/17		Fine day. Battalion at Musketry on "A" range near road to ST. OMER.	yes
	14/6/17		Fine day. Training of boys & Specialists. Miniature range practise, blotting & hit inspection	yes
	15/6/17		Warm day. Training of Lewis Gunners & Signallers. Company schemes & Field training	yes
	16/6/17		Good day. boys at Field Training. Ceremonial & usual training. Miniature range practise.	yes
	17/6/17		Warm day. SUNDAY. Church Parade. 100 men (25 from each Coy) went on Course to II nd Army School of Musketry. Rehearsal for Torchlight Tattoo in grounds at Battn. H.Q. & the Divisional Brass Band & Battalion Pipe Band gave selections. Draft of 44 men arrived.	yes

Army Form C. 2118.

WAR DIARY
or
INTELLIGENCE SUMMARY.
(Erase heading not required.)

Instructions regarding War Diaries and Intelligence Summaries are contained in F. S. Regs., Part II. and the Staff Manual respectively. Title pages will be prepared in manuscript.

Place	Date	Hour	Summary of Events and Information	Remarks and references to Appendices
LA PANNE	18/6/17		Warm day. Musketry practice on "B" range. Heavy thunderstorm in afternoon. Torchlight Tattoo took place in grounds of Battn. H.Q. Genl. Hunter, G.O.C. Division & representatives from other Battalions present. The tattoo was very successful & the grounds prettily decorated with Chinese lanterns. The Divisional Band & Battn. Pipe Band gave selections & dancing by pipers.	
	19/6/17		Showery day. Musketry practice. Training of specialists.	
	20/6/17		Wet day. Battalion attack practice.	
	21/6/17		Good day. Attack practice by half Battalions. Practice on advancing in Artillery formation & deployment. General Gough, Commanding 5th Army, watched the Battalion at practice.	
	22/6/17		Battalion marched from LA PANNE to LEDERZEELE via WATTEN arriving at 1.30 p.m.	
LEDERZEELE				
	23/6/17		Wet day but marching was good. No one fell out on the march.	
	24/6/17		Good day. Kit inspections & musketry instruction.	
	25/6/17		Sunday. Church Service. Draft of 20 other ranks from 6th Cameron Highrs. joined Battalion the training of boys in scouting. P.T. & B.F. & Musketry. Specialists under their own instructors.	
	26/6/17		Good day. Usual programme of training.	
	27/6/17		Good day. Battalion Route March.	
	28/6/17		Wet day. Training of boys & specialists. Draft of 2 Officers & 12.5 other ranks joined Battn. Officers were 2 Lts. F.A. HARROP & G. ROBSON.	
	29/6/17		Good day. Inspection of Draft. Officers & Sergeants paraded under Major Ind. A draft of 20 other ranks arrival. Battalion less Officers & Sergeants, route march. Officers & NCO's Specialists under their own instructors.	
	30/6/17		Wet day. Boys at field training to specialists under their own instructors.	

(Confidential)

War Diary

of

4th Battn. Seaforth Highlanders.

(Volume 34)

from 1st. July 1917.

to 31st. July 1917.

Army Form C. 2118.

WAR DIARY or INTELLIGENCE SUMMARY
(Erase heading not required.)

Instructions regarding War Diaries and Intelligence Summaries are contained in F. S. Regs., Part II. and the Staff Manual respectively. Title Pages will be prepared in manuscript.

Place	Date	Hour	Summary of Events and Information	Remarks and references to Appendices
LEDERZEELE	1st July		Sunday. Battalion in billets at LEDERZEELE. Church Service. AP	
	2nd "		Fine day. Training of Companies & Specialists. AP	
	3rd "		do. Baths at LE BEERSTACKE. AP	
	4th "		Dull day. Battalion Attack practice on ST. MOMELIN Training Area. AP	
	5th "		Good day. Battalion Attack practice. Baths. AP	
	6th "		Warm day. Attack practice. AP	
	7th "		Fine day. Company Training. AP	
	8th "		Wet day. Company Training. Gas helmet inspection. AP	
	9th "		Dull day. Church Service. AP	
"E" Camp near POPERINGHE A 30 Central			Dull day. The Battalion marched to ST. OMER & entrained at 9 a.m. & arrived at POPERINGHE about 2 p.m. & detrained there. Marched from POPERINGHE Station to E Camp about 3 kilometres away. The enemy shelled the huts "surrounding" intermittently & exploded an ammunition dump near the Camp. We had 6 men wounded. AP	
TRENCHES	10th "		Dull day. 2 Lt. W.N. Collins was slightly wounded by shrapnel. Battalion relieved 6th Gordons in the line to the left of YPRES. Nos. 1 & 4 Coys in the front line & Nos. 2 & 3 Coys in Support. Headquarters at LANCASHIRE FARM. Enemy artillery active. AP	
	11th "		Good day. Enemy artillery fairly active. AP	
"E" Camp A 30 Central	12th "		Good day & very warm. Battalion was relieved by 4th Gordons & came back to E Camp at A 30 Central. We had 2 men killed & 6 wounded during tour in the line. MP	
HOUTKERQUE	13th "		Battalion marched to HOUTKERQUE via PROVEN & WATOU & went into Camp near the Church. MP	
	14th "		Good day. Baths. Cleaning of clothing & equipment. Kit inspection. MP	
	15th "		Sunday. R.C. Church Parade. 2 Lt D.G.Y Clark joined Battalion from England. MP	

WAR DIARY or INTELLIGENCE SUMMARY

Army Form C. 2118.

Place	Date	Hour	Summary of Events and Information	Remarks and references to Appendices
HOUTKERQUE	16th July		Good day. Battalion Attack Practice. 2Lt. G.F. Clark & 20 men went to 'N' Camp for tent fitting.	
	17th.		Good day. Training of Companies & Specialists.	
	18th.		Dull day. -do-	
	19th.		Warm day. Battalion Attack Practice. -do-	
	20th.		Warm day. Battalion route march via HERZEELE, BAMBECQUE & return. A Draft of 52 men arrived. -do-	
	21st "		Warm day. Training of Companies in digging, deploying, Artillery formation etc. Specialist Classes in Bombing & Signalling. -do-	
	22nd.		Warm day. Battalion marched from HOUTKERQUE at 5 am via WATOU & POPERINGHE & arrived at WINDMILL Camp (A.17.d.) about 10.30.am. Captn. R. Truslove was appointed Staff Captain of 153rd Infantry Brigade. Major M. Johnson, 4th K.O.S.B's. joined the Battalion from England. -do-	
WINDMILL CAMP (A.17.d.)	23rd "		Warm day. Companies at Physical Training & visit to model trenches. -do-	
	24th.		Good day. -do- A Working party of 1 2 Officers & 100 men were supplied for carrying oil drums to front line & were shelled with gas shells, causing arrival to be gassed & 1 man wounded. A French aeroplane came down near the Camp. -do-	
	25th "		Wet day. Physical Training & Bayonet fighting. Aeroplanes active. -do-	
	26th.		Good day. Presbyterian Church Service. Captn. L.H. Harris appointed Adjutant of Advanced Divisional Reinforcement Depot & R.S.M. Anderson as Sergeant Major.	
			1 Officer & 100 men on carrying party with oil drums. -do-	

Army Form C. 2118.

WAR DIARY
or
INTELLIGENCE SUMMARY
(Erase heading not required.)

Instructions regarding War Diaries and Intelligence Summaries are contained in F. S. Regs., Part II. and the Staff Manual respectively. Title Pages will be prepared in manuscript.

Place	Date	Hour	Summary of Events and Information	Remarks and references to Appendices
WINDMILL CAMP (A.19.d.)	27th July		Good day. P.T. & B.F. Aeroplane active. Enemy aeroplanes came over about 11 p.m. flying low & dropped surrounding camps & forced machine guns on roads etc. but we had no casualties.	
	28th		Warm day. P.T. & B.F. Our Heavy Artillery active. Enemy aeroplane again came over in the darkness & dropped bomb at the neighbourhood.	
	29th		Wet day. Church service. Our Artillery very active during the day.	
	30th		Dull day. Battalion moved into position of assembly at Canal Bank.	
	31st		Dull day. Remained at Canal Bank in reserve.	

[signature]
LIEUT. COLONEL
COMDG. 1/4th BN. SEAFORTH HIGHRS.

Confidential

War Diary
of
1/4th Battalion Seaforth Highlanders

(Volume 35)

from 1st August 1917.

to 31st August 1917.

WAR DIARY
or
INTELLIGENCE SUMMARY

(Erase heading not required.)

Army Form C. 2118.

Instructions regarding War Diaries and Intelligence Summaries are contained in F.S. Regs., Part II. and the Staff Manual respectively. Title Pages will be prepared in manuscript.

Place	Date	Hour	Summary of Events and Information	Remarks and references to Appendices
YSER CANAL BANK	1/8/17		Very wet day & ground very muddy. The Battalion moved up from the dugouts on the YSER CANAL BANK and relieved the 153-rd Infantry Brigade on the GREEN LINE (WEST of RIVER STEENBECK) to which they had advanced during the attack on the previous day about 2 miles beyond our old front line. Nos. 1 & 2 companies held the front line, Nos. 3 & 4 companies in Support & Headquarters in GOURNIER FARM. During the relief the S.O.S. signal went up from the Division on our left (38 H. Welsh Division) & our own and the enemy guns opened a heavy barrage, causing several casualties among our men. 2 Lt M MURRAY was wounded slightly.	No. 4 Coy northern - inter wing
FRONT LINE TRENCHES South of LANGEMARCK	2/8/17		On our right 9th Royal Scots & on the left 58th (Welsh) Division. Our front line ran along the road WEST of the River STEENBECK. A full wet day. Our own & enemy artillery were active all day, Headquarters & surroundings being shelled at intervals. Posts were established by Nos. 1 & 2 Coys & the Sniping section across the River STEENBECK. Many wounded German prisoners were brought in.	
	3/8/17		Weather slightly better, but the ground still wet & muddy. Walking difficult owing to large number of shell holes. Captn. P.B. MACINTYRE, Brigade Transport Officer, one of our original Officers was wounded by a shell at the CANAL BANK and died of wounds.	

Army Form C. 2118.

WAR DIARY or INTELLIGENCE SUMMARY

(Erase heading not required.)

Instructions regarding War Diaries and Intelligence Summaries are contained in F. S. Regs., Part II. and the Staff Manual respectively. Title Pages will be prepared in manuscript.

Place	Date	Hour	Summary of Events and Information	Remarks and references to Appendices
FRONT LINE TRENCHES SOUTH OF LANGEMARCK.	4/8/17		Bright day. Aeroplane & Artillery active on both sides. The Battalion was relieved by 4th London Highlanders & went back to the dugouts on CANAL BANK previously occupied by us before the attack. No. 3 Coy went to HINDENBURG FARM. in the old German lines. Casualties during the tour in the line were 1 Officer Wounded (2 Lt. M. MURRAY). Other Ranks Killed 20 Wounded 87 Missing 1 Wounded (gas) 1 Died of Wounds 5.	
YSER CANAL BANK.	5/8/17		Bright warm day. The Battalion moved to dugouts further right along the CANAL BANK to make room for a Battalion of new Division. German aeroplane were active & bombed Brigade Advanced Transport Camp at HOSPITAL FARM. causing casualties among men & horses. Our guns bombarded heavily about 10 p.m. for nearly an hour.	
HUTS A 30 central (Sheet 28 NW)	6/8/17		Good day. The Battalion was relieved by 9th Duke of Wellingtons Regt & went back to huts at A 30 central (Sheet 28 N.W.)	
	7/8/17		Good day. Resting & cleaning up & kit inspections. R.S.M. J. Smith took over the duties of R.S.M.	
'N' Camp ST JANSTER BIEZEN	8/8/17		Good day. The Battalion marched from camp at 5 am to camp at ST. JANSTER BIEZEN about 2 miles behind POPERINGHE.	
ST JANSTER BIEZEN	9/8/17		Wet day. Cleaning of equipment & clothing.	

WAR DIARY or INTELLIGENCE SUMMARY

Army Form C. 2118.

Place	Date	Hour	Summary of Events and Information	Remarks and references to Appendices
HELVELINGHEM	10/8/17		Good day. The Battalion marched to PROVEN Station & entrained at 8 a.m. & arrived at WATTEN about 3 p.m. Marched from WATTEN Station to HELVELINGHEM & went into billets there. M.J	
	11/8/17		Good day. 3 hours training in Physical Exercises, Bayonet fighting & musketry. M.J	
	12/8/17		Sunday. Church Parade. M.J	
	13/8/17		Good day. Bath at EPERLECQUES. Rifle inspection. Company training. Lieut. Moore & 2.Lt. FINLAYSON & 10 men joined the Battalion. M.J	
	14/8/17		Good day. Musketry practice. M.J	
	15/8/17		Good day. Brigade Attack Scheme. M.J	
	16/8/17		Good day. Training of Companies & Specialists. M.J	
	17/8/17		Good day. Do. M.J	
	18/8/17		Do.	
	19/8/17		Sunday. Church Service. M.J	
	20/8/17		Good day. Training of Companies & Specialists. 2 Lt. N. SUTHERLAND & 14 O.R. men & reinforcements joined the Battalion. M.J	
	21/8/17		Good day. Training of Companies. Inspection of Drafts by C.O. M.J	

WAR DIARY or INTELLIGENCE SUMMARY

Army Form C. 2118.

Place	Date	Hour	Summary of Events and Information	Remarks and references to Appendices
NELVELING HEM.	22/8/17		Good day. Training of Companies & Specialists. Bathing in LA PANNE CANAL.	M.J.
CAMP	23/8/17		Wet day. Battalion marched to WATTEN Station & went by train at 9.30 p.m. to ABEELE Station arriving at 1.30 a.m. Marched from there to Huts at ST JANSTER BIEZEN.	M.J.
ST. JANSTER BIEZEN.	24/8/17		Cold day & very strong wind.	M.J.
	25/8/17		Good day. Training of Companies & Specialists.	M.J.
	26/8/17		Good day. Trench Tennis. Baths.	M.J.
	27/8/17		Wet day. Training of Companies & Specialists.	M.J.
	28/8/17		Do.	M.J.
MURAT CAMP	29/8/14	11.30 a.m.	Dull day. Battalion marched to MURAT CAMP near CANAL BANK arriving at 11.30 a.m.	M.J.
	30/8/17		Dull day. Companies at Attack Practice. Release of Lewis Gunners & Signallers training.	M.J.
	31/8/17		Dull day. Lieut. Col. J.L. Unthank took over command of 154th Infantry Brigade on Brigadier General Hamilton going on leave. Enemy aeroplane came over about 10 p.m. at night & dropped bombs in the neighbourhood. It was hit by our Lewis Guns & fell about a mile away.	M.J.

M. Jobson Major
Comdg 1/4 th Seaforth Highlanders

154/51

Confidential
War Diary
of
1/4th Battn. Seaforth Highlanders
Volume 36

from 1st September 1917.

to 30th September 1917.

Army Form C. 2118.

WAR DIARY
or
INTELLIGENCE SUMMARY.
(Erase heading not required.)

Instructions regarding War Diaries and Intelligence Summaries are contained in F. S. Regs., Part II. and the Staff Manual respectively. Title pages will be prepared in manuscript.

Place	Date	Hour	Summary of Events and Information	Remarks and references to Appendices
MURAT CAMP	1/9/17		The Battalion lay in camp at MURAT CAMP behind YSER CANAL near BRIELEN. Warm day. Training of Companies & Specialists.	m.f.
	2/9/17		Sunday. Wet day. Divine Service. 2 Officers & 100 men supplied for work on new musketry range under R.E. & 25 men on sanitary work at CANAL BANK. Enemy aeroplanes dropped bombs in the neighbourhood of Camp.	m.f.
	3/9/17		Good day. Training of Companies & Specialists continued. Enemy shelled neighbourhood of the Camp. German aeroplane flew over during the night & landed the near area (Ref map 28 N.W. 5 a - A 30 Central)	m.f.
DIRTY BUCKET CAMP (Ref. to map Sheet 28 NW)	4/9/17		Warm day. The Battalion moved to DIRTY BUCKET CAMP (Ref. map 28 N.W. 5 a - A 30 Central) arriving at 11 a.m. Working parties of 50 men & 10 men on salvage work were supplied to the CANAL BANK and during the night 9 dropped bombs. Enemy aeroplanes again came over during the night.	m.f.
	5/9/17		Good day. Baths were allotted to the Battalion's Companies at practice in consolidating shell holes. Enemy aeroplanes again dropped bombs during the night.	m.f.
	6/9/17		Warm day. The Battalion moved up and relieved the 5th Seaforths in the front line trenches near LANGEMARCK.	m.f.
FRONT LINE TRENCHES near LANGEMARCK	7/9/17		Dull day. Nothing unusual happened.	m.f.
	8/9/17		Warm day. Artillery active on both sides. 2 Lt DADDISON wounded. The Battalion was relieved & came back to Brigade reserve at YSER CANAL BANK.	m.f.
YSER CANAL BANK	9/9/17		Good day. Nothing unusual occurred.	m.f.
	10/9/17		do	do
	11/9/17			

WAR DIARY
or
INTELLIGENCE SUMMARY.
(Erase heading not required.)

Army Form C. 2118.

Place	Date	Hour	Summary of Events and Information	Remarks and references to Appendices
SIEGE CAMP	12/9/17		The Battalion was relieved by 7th Black Watch and came back to SIEGE CAMP near ELVERDINGHE. Lieut. Col. Whitbank rejoined the Battalion from Brigade Headquarters on the return of Brig. Genl. Hamilton. M.J.	
	13/9/17		Good day. Resting & cleaning up & clothing etc. A working party of 80 men was supplied erecting duckwalks around tents in Camp for protection from bombs. M.J.	
	14/9/17		Dull day. Working party supplied the same as yesterday. Bombers and Lewis Gunners of No 1 Coy. Training under Instructor. M.J.	
	15/9/17		Good day. Baths near Camp were used by the Battalion. Training of Companies & Specialists. Enemy aeroplanes dropped bombs in the next camp causing some casualties. The camp was shelled during the night 2 men being killed. M.J.	
	16/9/17		Good day. Training of Companies in Attack practice & stabbeats under their own Instructor. Aeroplane activity on both sides. M.J.	
	17/9/17		Dull day. Attack practice carried out. M.J.	
	18/9/17		Dull day. The Battalion took part in attack practice by the whole Brigade. M.J.	
	19/9/17		Good day. Marched from SIEGE Camp into assembly position leaving Camp at 8.30 p.m. An attack on the LANGEMARCK - S(TEEN)BEEK System takes place tomorrow. M.J.	
ASSEMBLY POSITIONS WEST OF LANGEMARCK	20/9/17	3.30am	All Companies in Assembly positions M.J. (All map references are ref. map POELCAPPELLE R. 1/10,000)	

Army Form C. 2118.

WAR DIARY
or
~~INTELLIGENCE SUMMARY.~~
(Erase heading not required.)

Instructions regarding War Diaries and Intelligence Summaries are contained in F. S. Regs., Part II. and the Staff Manual respectively. Title pages will be prepared in manuscript.

Place	Date	Hour	Summary of Events and Information	Remarks and references to Appendices
WEST OF LANGEMARCK	20/9/17	5.40 a.m.	Attack commenced. WHITE HOUSE occupied without opposition. PHEASANT TRENCH very strongly held. Trench intact & captured with very little opposition on left very fierce fighting on right.	
		6.10 a.m.	CEMETERY and PHEASANT FARM reported captured; large number of Germans killed; very few prisoners taken. On left all objectives taken on time. Attack delayed on right owing to strong opposition by bombing & M.G. fire from concrete houses. 1 platoon of left Company wheeled to right to support attack of right Company.	
		6.28 a.m.	Reported all objectives captured.	
		6.50 a.m.	Ammunition sent up.	
		9 a.m.	Prisoner reported enemy would counter attack immediately from Sof POELCAPPELLE. Ordered up 2 platoons of No. 1 Coy. that were in reserve.	
		9.30 a.m.	12th R.B. on left reported their line ran U.24.b.9.3 to U.23.d.9.4 and left 13m. held up by Machine gun fire from EAGLE TRENCH (U.23.d.9.5.7.0) Formed defensive flank.	
		4.45 p.m.	Informed by 4th Gordons they were attacked on their right and had given way to a line about 100 yards in front of MALTA HOUSE. M.J.	

WAR DIARY
or
INTELLIGENCE SUMMARY.
(Erase heading not required.)

Army Form C. 2118.

Place	Date	Hour	Summary of Events and Information	Remarks and references to Appendices
WEST OF LANGEMARCK	20/9/17	4.55 p.m.	Left Coy. reported small parties of the 4th Gordons withdrawing. 11 hostile aeroplanes flew low over our own lines between 3.45 p.m. & 4.15 p.m. Enemy shelling heavy since 3.45 p.m.	
		6.10 p.m.	Reported that enemy had made a strong counter attack driving in the forward posts.	
		6.30 p.m.	Saw line withdrawing & sent up reinforcements. Posted 1 M.G. at WHITE HOUSE.	
		6.50 p.m.	Reported holding line in advance of WHITE HOUSE – PHEASANT FARM – CEMETERY on left. Two platoons counter attacked on right and re-established the line driving the enemy back into our barrage & inflicting heavy casualties.	
			Nothing of incidents occurred during the night. A.J.	
	21/9/17		Nothing of incidents occurred until 6 p.m. when Germans were seen to be massing for a counter attack. Heavy barrage opened by both sides.	
		7.30 p.m.	It was reported no further signs of attack and situation had resumed normality.	
			Relieved by 5th K.O.S.B.s. Bns during the night & moved back to SIEGE Camp. A.J.	

Army Form C. 2118.

WAR DIARY or INTELLIGENCE SUMMARY

(Erase heading not required.)

Place	Date	Hour	Summary of Events and Information	Remarks and references to Appendices
WEST OF LANGEMARCK	21/9/17		Casualties during the operation from 19th to 23rd inst.:- Killed – 2 Lieuts. J.A. MACKENZIE, D.I.C. CLARK, G. ROBSON, J.T. JENKINS, Wounded Capt. D.B.M. JACKSON, 2 Lieuts. P.H. BALLANTYNE, F.A. HARROP, A. MUNRO. Other ranks Killed 41, Wounded 153, Missing 15. M.J.	
SIEGE Camp	22/9/17		Battn. Resting & cleaning up. M.J.	
	23/9/17		Sunday. Church Services. M.J.	
	24/9/17		Colonel Unthank went on leave & Major Johren took over command of the Battn. M.J. Battn. marched to billets in POPERINGHE. M.J.	
POPERINGHE	25/9/17		A draft of 162 men joined the Battn. M.J.	
	26/9/17		Draft of 130 men from 2/4th Seaforths arrived. M.J.	
	27/9/17		Rifle inspections &c. M.J.	
	28/9/17		Marched from POPERINGHE at 9.30 p.m. & entrained at HOUPOUTRE Station at 10.30 p.m. & arrived at BAPAUME at 10.30 a.m. next day. M.J.	
COURCELLES	29/9/17		Marched from BAPAUME to huts near COURCELLES. M.J.	
	30/9/17		Sunday. Church Services. M.J.	

M. Johren Major.
Comdg. 1/c Seaforth H'ghrs.

(Confidential)

War Diary

of

4th. Bn. Seaforth Highlanders.

(Volume 37)

from 1st October 1917 to 31st October 1917.

Army Form C. 2118.

WAR DIARY
or
INTELLIGENCE SUMMARY

(Erase heading not required.)

Instructions regarding War Diaries and Intelligence Summaries are contained in F.S. Regs., Part II. and the Staff Manual respectively. Title Pages will be prepared in manuscript.

Place	Date	Hour	Summary of Events and Information	Remarks and references to Appendices
COURCELLES LE-COMTE	1/10/17		Battn. in huts at COURCELLES about 8 kilos N.W. of BAPAUME. Coys training in musketry Gas helmet drill etc. Battn at COURCELLES.	
	2/10/17		Good day. Usual training of bombers & specialists. Specialists under their own instructors. Coys training in musketry, Physical training etc. Lieut. E.A. Mackintosh, 2 Lieuts R.J. Gordon, H. Paterson & E.J. Martin joined Battn.	
	3/10/17		Warm day. Coys at musketry, Physical training etc.	
	4/10/17		Good day. Usual training programme. A football match between Officers & Sergeants of the Battn played in one goal each.	
	5/10/17		Battn. left Camp at COURCELLES-le-COMTE at 8 a.m. & embussed on the COURCELLES-HAMELINCOURT Road and were taken to a point M 30 a.0.9 (Ref Map 51.B.S.W.) From there Battn. marched to the trenches and relieved the 5th YORKS in the front line, left sector of the Brigade between GUEMAPPE & VIS-EN-ARTOIS. Nos 1 & 2 Coys in front line, No. 4 in support & No 3 in Reserve at MARLIERE Dump. 9th Royal Scots on right & 12 th Div on left.	
FRONT LINE Trenches N.W. of QUEMAPPE	6/10/17		Line extremely quiet. Very quiet. Wet & cold day.	
	7/10/17		Very quiet day. Artillery a little more active on both sides. A raid by Division on left in the evening drew enemy retaliation on our front & 2 Lt O.B. SIMPSON & 2 O.R. were killed by shell fire in SOUTHERN AVENUE.	

WAR DIARY
or
INTELLIGENCE SUMMARY

Army Form C. 2118.

Place	Date	Hour	Summary of Events and Information	Remarks and references to Appendices
FRONT LINE	8/10/17		Wet day. Fairly quiet on both sides.	
	9/10/17		Wet day. Nos. 3 & 4 coys relieved Nos. 1 & 2 coys in front line; Enemy shelled CAVALRY Trench immediately after relief, killing 1 man & wounding 4.	
	10/10/17		Fine day. Aerial activity. One E.A. brought down.	
	11/10/17		Fine day. Aeroplanes again active. One E.A. flew very low over our lines about 8.30 a.m.	
	12/10/17		Wet day. Enemy raided one of our forward posts about 4.30 a.m. Raid was preceded by 6 T.M. bombardment. Bombs were thrown into D.D. front & some of our men were wounded. Some dead Germans were left in our wire & one wounded prisoner was taken by us. None of our men are missing. The Royal Scots on right were also raided & suffered some casualties, having 1 man missing.	
CARLISLE Huts	13/10/17		Bath. was relieved by 7th A. & S. Hrs.; Nos. 1 & 2 Coys went to shelters vacated by 4th Gordons near MARLIERE Farm; Nos. 3, 4 & 9 Battn. H.Q. to CARLISLE Huts. near ARRAS-BAUPAUME Road.	
	14/10/17		Sunday. Church Services. Cleaning up. Our artillery bombarded enemy trenches about 5 p.m. lasting half an hour.	
	15/10/17		Fine day. Rifle inspection. Baths in Camp. Capt. Geo. Kaufman, Lieuts. Macaulay, Macgregor and 2/Lts. Roberts and McMinnis joined Battalion.	

Army Form C. 2118.

WAR DIARY
or
INTELLIGENCE SUMMARY

(Erase heading not required.)

Instructions regarding War Diaries and Intelligence Summaries are contained in F. S. Regs., Part II. and the Staff Manual respectively. Title Pages will be prepared in manuscript.

Place	Date	Hour	Summary of Events and Information	Remarks and references to Appendices
CARLISLE Huts	16/10/17		Good day. Training of Coys & Specialists, Musketry etc.	
	17/10/17		do	Yes
	18/10/17		do	Yes
	19/10/17		do	Yes
	20/10/17		Fine day. Nos. 3 & 4 Coys on Route March. Specialists on Rifle ranges. 1. Football League the Battn. lost to 9th. Black Watch	Yes
FRONT LINE Trenches	21/10/17		Battn relieved 9th A&SH in the front line. Enemy shelled our trenches immediately after relief. Nos. 1 & 2 Coys in front line, No. 3 Coy in Support & No 4 Coy in Reserve. 1 O.R. was killed & 1 wounded	Yes
	22/10/17		Dull day. Line very quiet	Yes
	23/10/17		Dull day. Our artillery was active in the afternoon.	Yes
	24/10/17		Fine day. Quiet on our front. Aeroplanes active	Yes
	25/10/17		do	Yes
	26/10/17		do. Captn. H.P.T. Gray rejoined the Battn. from Base duty	Yes
	27/10/17		do	Yes
IZEL-LES HAMEAUX	28/10/17		Cold day, very frosty. Battn. was relieved by 2nd Bn. Lanc. Regt, embussed at MERCATEL cross Roads on ARRAS- BAPAUME Road & arrived at billets in IZEL-LES HAMEAUX	Yes

Army Form C. 2118.

WAR DIARY
or
INTELLIGENCE SUMMARY

(Erase heading not required.)

Instructions regarding War Diaries and Intelligence Summaries are contained in F. S. Regs., Part II. and the Staff Manual respectively. Title Pages will be prepared in manuscript.

Place	Date	Hour	Summary of Events and Information	Remarks and references to Appendices
IZEL - LES - HAMEAUX	28/10/17		Details went by train & Transport by road. Col Writhard returned from Brigade H.Q.	yes yes
	29/10/17		Dull day. Cleaning up. Kit inspections.	
	30/10/17		Wet day. Training of Coys. & Specialists. Captn. A.K. Fraser, 2 Lts J. Christie & H.C. Bedsont & 15 other ranks joined Battn.	yes yes
	31/10/17		Good day. Training of Coys. & Specialists.	yes

J. Wilkinson Lt Col
Com'g 4/ Suffolk R.

1 - 11 - 17.

154th Brigade.

51st Division.

4th BATTALION

SEAFORTH HIGHLANDERS

NOVEMBER 1917.

Attached:-

Report on Operations at Cambrai.

(CONFIDENTIAL.)

WAR DIARY OF

4TH. BATTALION SEAFORTH HIGHLANDERS.

(VOLUME 38.)

FROM 1st. November 1917. TO 30th. November 1917.

Army Form C. 2118.

WAR DIARY
INTELLIGENCE SUMMARY
(Erase heading not required.)

Instructions regarding War Diaries and Intelligence Summaries are contained in F. S. Regs., Part II. and the Staff Manual respectively. Title Pages will be prepared in manuscript.

Place	Date	Hour	Summary of Events and Information	Remarks and references to Appendices
IZEL - LE HAMEAUX	1/11/17		Battn in billets at IZEL-LE-HAMEAUX. Training of Companies & Specialists.	See
	2/11/17		Full day. Battn. Usual training programme. Inter-Coy football matches.	See
	3/11/17		Full day. Battalion route march. Football in afternoon.	See
	4/11/17		Full day. Sunday. Church service.	See
	5/11/17		Full day. Baths. Training of Coys. & Specialists.	See
	6/11/17		do. 2/Lt. N.F. Swan joined Battalion	See
	7/11/17		do.	See
	8/11/17		do. Battn. Cross Country Race. No 2 Coy. won.	See
	9/11/17		do. Training of Coys. & Specialists as usual.	See
	10/11/17		do. Brigade Boxing Contest	See
	11/11/17		Sunday. Church Parade. A concert was given by the Battn. Officers at Divisional Theatre.	See
	12/11/17		Good day. Lieut. C. Ferguson bombing. 17th Corps presented medal Ribbons to recipients of honour gained at YPRES.	See
	13/11/17		Bright day. Anniversary of the capture of BEAUMONT HAMEL by the 51st (Highland) Division. Brigade Sports at NOEULLE-VION. The day was observed as a holiday. Special dinners served to the men & entertainment	See

2449 Wt. W14957/M90 750,000 1/16 J.B.C. & A. Forms/C.2118/12.

Army Form C. 2118.

WAR DIARY
or
INTELLIGENCE SUMMARY

(Erase heading not required.)

Instructions regarding War Diaries and Intelligence Summaries are contained in F. S. Regs., Part II. and the Staff Manual respectively. Title Pages will be prepared in manuscript.

Place	Date	Hour	Summary of Events and Information	Remarks and references to Appendices
IZEL-LE-HAMEAUX	13/11/17		at the Divisional Theatre in the evening.	yes
	14/11/17		Full day. Training of Coys. & Specialists as usual.	yes
	15/11/17		Full day. Training of Coys. for the attack. Specialist classes as usual.	yes
	16/11/17		Full day. Organising of Coys. into complete sections & platoons. Transport moved by road to BOISLEUX-AU-MONT leaving about 10 p.m.	yes
			Battalion (less surplus personnel who remained at IZEL-LE-HAMEAUX)	yes
BAPAUME	17/11/17		marched to BEAUMETZ & entrained there about 6 p.m. arriving at BAPAUME station at 9 p.m. & went into tents in that town for the night.	yes
			Battn. marched by road to RAILWAY CAMP, LECHELLE leaving BAPAUME at 5 p.m. & arriving in camp about 9.30 p.m.	yes
LECHELLE	18/11/17		Full day. Resting & completing arrangements for attack.	yes
	19/11/17		Transport moved to field between NEUVILLE & METZ. An attack taken place tomorrow on the CANTAING trench system. Reference map. 57.C.S.E.	yes
			Battalion moved up to billets in METZ.	yes
METZ	20/11/17	10 a.m.	Battn. formed up in position outside village.	yes
		4.30 p.m.	Allowed to return to billets.	yes
			The 152 nd. & 153 rd Infantry Brigades had attacked the German front line system along with the 6th & 51st divisions & captured it. 154 th Infantry Brigade with Seaforths & H.L.Is in Brigade Reserve.	yes

WAR DIARY
or
INTELLIGENCE SUMMARY

(Erase heading not required.)

Army Form C.2.

Instructions regarding War Diaries and Intelligence Summaries are contained in F.S. Regs., Part II. and the Staff Manual respectively. Title Pages will be prepared in manuscript.

Place	Date	Hour	Summary of Events and Information	Remarks and references to Appendices
	21/11/17	11 a.m.	Battn. left METZ to take up position in original German front line system.	See
		1.30 a.m.	moved up to original German front line	See
		9.15 a.m.	Battalion assembled at N.9.a.b.5. & moved past FLESQUIERES along to LA JUSTICE. No. 4 company extended to fill gap between 9th & 9th K.O.Y.L.I. and 62nd Division. Advance stopped by Machine Gun fire from the CANTAING LINE and ANNEUX	See
		12 noon	Tanks arrived and advance resumed. No. 1 Company took the CANTAING LINE. Nos. 2 & 4 companies took CANTAING MILL & outskirts of CANTAING. Advance continued along with Tanks & captured FONTAINE - NOTRE - DAME. Consolidated in posts to South & East of the village. 7th A & S. Highrs on North side. The night was quiet.	See See See
	22/11/17	5.30 a.m.	No. 3 Company moved up to relieve 7th A & S Highrs in FONTAINE	See
		6.15 a.m.	Battn. Headquarters moved up to the village of FONTAINE. A fleet of enemy aeroplanes flew over the village very low & remained overhead for about 3 hours firing at our men. The S.O.S. was sent up but Germans were massing troops behind their lines. Enemy barrage & our Artillery failed to prepare to it & did not open fire.	See See
		9.30 a.m.	a counter attack from BOURLON WOOD, CAMBRAI ROAD & LA FOLIE WOOD, coming forward in several waves in extended order. No supports arrived, the supply	See

WAR DIARY
or
INTELLIGENCE SUMMARY

Army Form C. 2118.

Place	Date	Hour	Summary of Events and Information	Remarks and references to Appendices
	22/11/17	*	of ammunition & bombs became exhausted & after a bitter resistance & greatly outnumbered our men had to evacuate the village & retired a few hundred yards on the other side. No 3 Company retired to SUNKEN Road in F.21.C. The remainder of Battalion to SUNKEN Road in F.21.b.9.d. Some of our wounded who were too badly wounded to move had to be left in the village and Captn. & Adjutant T H PEVERELL who had gone up to take charge in the front line was wounded & refusing to be taken back was last seen firing at the advancing enemy. Captn. A.K.FRASER, O.C. No 3 Coy was also wounded in trying to check the enemy and had to be left behind.	
		2.30 p.m.	Battn. formed a defensive flank and dug in.	
		10.30 p.m.	Battn. relieved by 7th Black Watch & came back to FLESQUIERES.	
			Casualties. K/Feb. 10 Officers and 308 other ranks.	
			Officers - Killed. Captn. S.M.McMONNIES, 2 Lt. S.M.McMONNIES, 2 Lt. N.F.SWAN., 2 Lt. H PATERSON. WOUNDED Captn. A.M.McDONALD, Lieut. E.A.MACKINTOSH, Lieut. N.SUTHERLAND, Captn. H.R.T.GRAY, Lieut. D.E.F.MAC GREGOR. WOUNDED and MISSING Captn. & Adjutant T.H.PEVERELL. Captn. A.K.FRASER. Other Ranks killed 30 Wounded 192 Missing 86.	
METZ	23/11/17		Battn. relieved from FLESQUIERES. Went back to old billets in METZ.	

WAR DIARY
or
INTELLIGENCE SUMMARY

(Erase heading not required.)

Army Form C. 2118.

Place	Date	Hour	Summary of Events and Information	Remarks and references to Appendices
METZ	24/11/17		Battn. marched from METZ to railhead at YTRES and entrained there about 8 p.m. arriving at TREUX station and marched from there to billets in RIBEMONT arriving about 3 a.m.	
RIBEMONT	25/11/17		Very cold & dull weather. Resting & cleaning up.	See
	26/11/17		Dull wet day. Resting, cleaning up.	See
	27/11/17		Dull day. Cleaning up. Reorganising companies, platoons & sections.	See
	28/11/17		Dull day, Companies marched to Commanding Officer. Remainder of morning spent in physical training & Good day. Coys. training in attack & defence. Lewis Gun & Bombing Classes at 2.45 p.m. for the Battn. to be prepared to move in the evening to the forward area as the enemy had made a big attack & broken the line.	
	29/11/17		Good day but cold. Training of Coys. 9 Specialists. Orders were received	See
	30/11/17		The Battn. marched to EDGE HILL & entrained at 8 p.m. arriving at BAPAUME about 1 a.m. & marched from there by road to huts at ROCQUIGNY arriving about 5.30 a.m.	See

4TH. BATTALION SEAFORTH HIGHLANDERS.

NARRATIVE OF OPERATIONS.

FROM NOVEMBER 20TH. TO NOVEMBER 22ND. 1917.

4th. Battn. SEAFORTH HIGHLANDERS.

NARRATIVE OF OPERATIONS FROM NOVEMBER 20th. TILL NOVEMBER 22nd.

November 20th.
Marched from LECHELLES at 2.30 a.m. reaching METZ and going into Billets at 4.45 a.m. Gave men a rum ration and turned in. About 10.0 a.m. formed up outside Village and remained there rest of day till 4.30 p.m. when asked Brigade for permission to return to Billets which was granted and stayed there till 4.0 a.m. when marched to front line system, reporting move complete at 6.0 a.m.

Found 7th. A.& S. Hrs. still in possession.
At 6.30 a.m. moved forward to German front line system and with considerable difficulty assembled the Battalion on track in K.30.a. Then moved past right of FLESQUIERES past Beetroot Factory along road to LA JUSTICE. On reaching LA JUSTICE found Front Line of 153rd. Infantry Brigade, 7th. A.& S. Hrs. advancing on my left, 4th. Gordons reported about L.8.b.

Advanced No. 4 Company with left on LA JUSTICE - FONTAINE-NOTRE-DAME Road, connecting with 7th. A.& S.Hrs. and with orders to advance to Crest Line.

Enemy Machine Gun fire was now coming from ANNEUX from about L.2.c.8.6. and advance was stopped.

Position of Companies at this time was :-
No. 4 Coy. extended from about Road Junction North of LA JUSTICE through L.2.c.
No. 2 Company extended in L.2.c.
Nos. 1 & 3 Companies in column of fours on road between ORIVAL WOOD and LA JUSTICE.

I then detailed Captn. Macdonald, O.C.No. 1 Company to send a platoon to deal with hostile Machine Guns in L.2.c.8.6.
I pointed out position of guns to 2/Lieut. McMonnies and Sergt. Ross who proceeded to deal with them. They found 3 Machine Guns and drove them back into village of CANTAING, down Sunken Road in L.2.b.

The enemy retired fighting and unfortunately wounded Sergt.Ross through the arm with his last burst. This was the only casualty in a very well executed manoeuvre.

The position then remained stationary, the enemy were in strength in the CANTAING Line with at least 3 Machine Guns in CANTAING MILL. Later CANTAING was captured by Tanks, and shortly after Tanks arrived on our front and the advance resumed.

Order of Battle.
1 platoon of No. 1 Company on right.
No. 4 Company.
No. 1 Company less 1 platoon in support of 7th.A.& S.Hrs. on left of Road to FONTAINE.
No. 2 Company in support to No. 4 Company.
No. 3 Company in reserve.

As the advance progressed and the CANTAING Line fell No. 3 Company was moved up to F.25.b. and F.26.a. to form a defensive flank facing BOURLON WOOD and connecting with 2 platoons of 7th.A.& S.Hrs. in the CANTAING line in F.20.c. and 19 D.

CANTAING MILL was captured and one Anti-Tank Gun.
2 platoons of No. 4 Company swung round to right and helped in capture of CANTAING, later moving up to F.22.a. and reporting to Captn. HARRIS.

CAPTURE OF CANTAING LINE.

No.1 Company advancing with the Tanks had passed through the 7th. A.& S.Hrs., who were busy digging in and apparently had not received orders, and captured the CANTAING LINE.

The 7th. A.& S. Hrs. followed on, some with No. 1 Company and some behind and cleared the dugouts and rounded up prisoners.

Nos. 2 & 4 Companies had meanwhile taken the CANTAING MILL and captured 30 prisoners.

They then swung to the left and bombed dugouts in SUNKEN ROAD F.21c. connected their line and proceeded to advance.

POSITION. No. 1 Company on left of Road LA JUSTICE - FONTAINE.
NOs. 2 & 4 Companies intermixed on right.
The whole were now considerably in advance of the Tanks and suffered heavy casualties from BOURLON WOOD. Captn. Macdonald was killed about/

about/   2.

F.21.a.1.3. The Tanks arrived and advanced on village and put out of action all Machine Guns - Some prisoners were captured in a Trench being dug on South side of village.

7th. A.& S.Hrs. holding the left as far as the Station,(2 Companies and 3 platoons.)

4th. Seaforth Hrs. the right. (See Map.)

STRENGTH.
  No. 1 Company   47.
  No. 4 Company   40.
  No. 2 Company   76.

TIME.   9.0 p.m.

[margin note: O.C did not know there was till morning of 22nd. B'n knew nothing about the depletion of Coys till after the operations K.G.B]

I asked the Brigade Major for reinforcements and for ammunition and the Brigade Major arriving at Headquarters at LA JUSTICE at the time we discussed the matter. He told me that the 9th. Royal Scots were relieving the 4th. Gordons in CANTAING and were not available.

Later I received instructions from Brigade to arrange with O.C. 7th. A.& S.Hrs. that one of us was to take over front line and that a Squadron of K.E.H. would come up in the morning.

I arranged to move up my No. 3 Company to relieve his Company in FONTAINE, the position of this Company to be taken up by one of his Companies at present in SUNKEN ROAD F.21.c.

Guides were provided for 5.30 a.m. and were moving up at 6.a.m. I met my Company on Road in F.26.c.

At 5.30 a.m. I sent up Lieut. Campbell and Battalion Scouts to establish 4 observation Posts in F.9.c., F.9.d., F.10.c. And F.16.b. (on CAMBRAI ROAD.)

These were reported in position about 7.a.m.

at about 6.30 a.m. a fleet of 12 German aeroplanes appeared and circled over FONTAINE at a low altitude. I lined up my Headquarters in the Main Street and opened fire causing them to fly off at a higher altitude but they continued to circle round the whole morning till after 10.0 a.m., delaying the relief and causing considerable casualties to my No. 3 Company moving into position.

At about 9 a.m. one of our aeroplanes charged into the midst of them and engaged one at close quarters. He was pursued in the direction of CAMBRAI and lost sight of. Later 4 of our machines chased off one German and caused him to land behind our lines.

It was found impossible to relieve 2 platoons of 7th. A.& S.Hrs. Immediately on relief Germans were reported massing in BOURLON WOOD and later on the CAMBRAI ROAD.

At about 9.30 a.m. No. 3 Company fired the S.O.S. and about 20 Minutes later I ordered the S.O.S. at Headquarters in F. 15.d.3.4. Failing response I sent the F.O.O. off on a horse, having previously sent my groom to inform 7th. A.& S.Hrs, & Brigade of the situation.

The enemy now commenced to advance in 5 or 6 waves on lines shown by arrows on attached map.

He was at first stopped on CAMBRAI ROAD by No. 1 Company at house F.16.6.7.1. He then turned off into Railway Cutting and drove back posts at F.16.a.5.3. These retired to houses on Main CAMBRAI Road.

I then sent up 2 platoons of No. 4 Company South of village to fill gap about Railway Station. Immediately afterwards I sent my Adjutant up to CAMBRAI ROAD to take charge. I then fell in my Headquarters and advanced along main CAMBRAI ROAD.

I then met the 2 platoons of No.4 Company falling back and sent my R.S.M. to lead them back to Railway Station.

Proceeding up the Road I met Captn. Peverell falling back and sent him back and went myself to Railway Station.

I here found the enemy 200 yards off in great force and after holding in for afew minutes and finding him dressing as shown by arrow, fell back to position marked with an X F.15.d.5.7. and posted some of my Headquarters and a few of No. 4 Company to hold it and Road Junction F.15.d.25.65.

Here I met Captn. Fraser falling back with 1 Platoon and sent him back. He lined ~~him meanwhile lined~~ Road F.15.c.20.60. to F.15.c. 90.70.

Meanwhile Captn. Peverell was wounded at F.16.c.9.9. and as his party was now reduced to 2 men without ammunition he advised them to withdraw and leave him.

The left had now given way and Captn. Fraser formed his Company up along CAMBRAI ROAD in vicinity of Factory and eventually they retired to Sunken Road in F.21.c. He himself was shot through the

the   3.

Legs in the Main Street and left behind.

They suffered very heavy casualities in covering this ground. On the extreme right a Platoon of No.4 Company shot away all their ammunition whilst lying in Road LA FOLIE WOOD, inflicting heavy casualities on the Germans and then withdrew to Sunken Road in F.21.b &d. The enemy were now pouring over Main Road on both sides of my party and we withdrew slowly by a Church, shooting a few men on the way. On reaching the edge of the Village we found Germans advancing in 6 waves from the LA FOLIE ROAD about a 150 yards away and also South of the Factory. My party was now reduced to 6 men. We opened rapid fire for a minute and bolted for Sunken Road in F.21.b. under heavy cross fire at close quarters. Every man was now out of the Village, the M.O. had evacuated all the wounded in the Aid Post except 6, too badly wounded to move.

4 deserters including an Officer were left at Battalion H.Q. It was now 2.30 p.m.

The remnants of No.3 Company and some of No.4. Company were now with 7th. A.& S. Highlanders in Sunken Road F.21.c. and helping them to fire on enemy in BOURLON WOOD, and Trench South of Factory.

The 7th. A. & S. Highlanders had been firing throughout the day and inflicted heavy casualities on the enemy.

Nos. 2, 4 and 1 Companies lined Sunken Road in F.21.b.& d. in conjunction with Capt Maxwell's Company 9th. Royal Scots.

The enemy attempted no further advance on Left but advanced on Right.

We attempted a charge from Road in F.21.b. but the men were too beat to carry on and halted about a 100 yards from the enemy who had started to retire.

We then retired to the Road, reformed, formed a defensive flank to the Left with 2 Platoons of No.2 Company.

I placed Lieut. Campbell in command of the remnants of Nos. 1 and 4 Companies.

He advanced and dug in.

The enemy attempted a further advance but was driven back, suffering heavy casualities and he attempted to dig in.

Battalion was relieved in the dark and assembled in FLESQUIERES at about 1.30 a.m. 23rd. inst.

Total casualities 10 Officers and 308 other ranks.

Rations were brought up to the village of FONTAINE on night of 21st. and a cooker was placed at LA JUSTICE and provided tea to No. 3 Company on way out.

REMARKS.

1. Owing to the loss of all diaries and documents at Battalion H.Q. which were destroyed by hostile shell fire, no times can be regarded as accurate.

2. Machine Gun Company.

Assistance from Machine Gun Company appears to have been negligible The Machine Gun in CAMBRAI Road jambed twice and did little good.
Machine Guns on left.
One appears to have been fired from House from South of Factory. One or two of the others are reported to have been knocked out. After questioning carefully my Officers and N.C.Os. in No. 3 Coy. I cannot find that any fired on their front. The Machine Gun Officer is missing. I understand, they abandoned their guns and fled. were left behind Lieut. Stewart with guns in rear of FONTAINE removed it to FLESQUIERES.

This is incorrect. Lt Stewart & guns after withdrawing from village were in action in F.21.D till dark on 22nd K9B

3. ARTILLERY.

As No response was given to my numerous S.O.S., the Artillery F.O.O. was sent back on a horse and my Artillery Liaison Officer reported 1 Battery firing. This Battery inflicted casualties in Quarry in Q.9. and helped to repulse them. Casualties were inflicted on our own men in trench in Q.15.c. & Q.14 c.& b.

Heavy casualties were caused to the enemy in BOURLON WOOD

Cabane	Hut.
Cabaret, Cab¹	Inn.
Câble sous-marin	Submarine cable.
Calvaire, Cal^re	Calvary.
Canal de déssèchement	Drainage canal
" d'irrigation	Irrigation canal
Fab^e de caoutchouc	Rubber factory.
Carrière, Carr^e	Quarry.
" de gravier	Gravel-pit.
Caserne	Barracks.
Champ de courses	Race course.
" manœuvres	Drill ground.
" tir	Rifle range.
Chantier	Building yard.
" de construction	Ship yard Dock yard } Slip-way
Chapelle, Ch^le	Chapel.
Charbonnage	Colliery.
Château d'eau	Water tower.
Chaussée	Causeway.
Chemin de fer	Railway.
" " Ch^in	Highway.
Cheminée	Chimney.
Chêne	Oak tree.
Cimetière, Cim^re	Cemetery.
Clocher	Belfry.
Clouterie	Nail factory.
Colombier	Dove-cot.

Dynamitière, Dynam^re	Dynamite magazine.
Dynamiterie	Dynamite factory.
Ecluse	Sluice, Lock.
Education, Ec^n	Sluice.
Ecole	School.
Ecurie	Stable.
Eglise	Church.
Emaillerie	Enamel works.
Embarcadère, Emb^re	Landing-place.
Estaminet, Estam¹	inn.
Etang	Pond.
Fabrique, Fab^e	Factory.
Fab^e de produits chimiques	Chemical works.
Fab^e de faïence } Faïencerie	Pottery.
Ferme	Farm.
Filature, Fil^re	Spinning mill
Fonderie, Fond^e	Foundry.
Fontaine, Font^e	Spring, fountain.
Forêt	Forest
Forme de radoub	Dry dock.
Forge	Smithy.
Fosse	Mine, Pit.
Fossé	Moat, Ditch.
Four	Kiln.
" à chaux	Lime-kiln.

Hôpital	Hospital
Hôtel-de-Ville	Town hall.
Houillère	Colliery
Huilerie	Oil factory
Imprimerie, Impr^ie	Printing works.
Jetée	Pier.
Laminerie	Rolling mills.
Laigne } de haute marée	High water mark.
Laisse } de basse marée	Low " " "
Maison Forestière M^on F^re	Forester's house.
Malterie	Malt-house.
Marbrerie	Marble works.
Marais	Marsh.
Marais salant	Salt marsh.
Marché	Market.
Mare	Pool.
Meule	Rick.
Minaire	Mine.
Monastère	Monastery.
Moulin, M^in	Mill.
" à vapeur	Steam mill.
Mur	Wall.
" criblé	Loop-holed well.

Peuplier	Poplar tree.
Phare	Lighthouse.
Pilier, Pil^r	Pier.
Piste d'manœuvre	Drill ground.
Pompe	Pump.
Ponceau	Culvert.
Pont	Bridge.
" -levis	Drawbridge.
Poste de garde- station	Coast-guard station
Poterie	Pott.
Potager P^er	Pottery.
Poudrière, Poud^re	Powder magazine.
Magasin à poudre	
Puits	Water supply
" " artésien	Pit-head, Shaft, Well. Artesian well
" d'aérage ventilateur de sondage	Ventilating shaft Boring.
Quai aux bestiaux	Quay, Platform.
" " marchandises	Cattle platform.
dus	Goods platform.
Raccordement	Junction.
Raffinerie	Refinery.
" de sucre	Sugar refinery
Râperie	Beet-root factory.

4.

4. The Brigade was asked for reinforcements and a supply of ammunition on night of 21st. inst. No ammunition was sent up but a dump made in ORIVAL WOOD of no use to anybody.

This S.A.A. dump was formed at 12.30 pm on 21st — 50 boxes — Other dumps were then formed at LA JUSTICE & CANTAING

The Squadron of King Edwards Horse did not arrive and no ammunition arrived in FONTAINE on morning of 22nd. inst.

I would suggest that in future Pack Transport is left in the hands of Battalions.

5. AEROPLANES. *In morning 22nd S.A.A. was sent forward from LA JUSTICE by pack & hand & was of great value to some 4/Seaforths — RAB*

No attempt was made to prevent the Germans from having the mastery of the air.

One British plane gallantly attacked 12 with the natural result.

Four more eventually came up and chased off 1 German plane but without affecting the situation.

6. GENERAL.

The perimeter of FONTAINE is 3500 yards. To attempt to hold this with 400 men (The strength the Battalion was reduced to) was impossible to repel a determined Counter attack. It only enabled a light line of out-posts to be established.

The ground rises in front of the village to the North and is much broken and allows a very short field of fire.
Connection was found impossible even between posts.
When once the line was broken no supports were available beyond moving up the 2 platoons covering the right rear and Battalion H.Q.

The men were much disheartened by :-

1. Low flying enemy planes (Causing severe casualties.)
2. No adequate Artillery support.
3. Seeing troops withdrawing in rear. *(I don't know who this refers to?)*

Most of the Lewis Gun teams had fired considerably the day before and ran out of ammunition early in the action.

On the whole the resistance put up was considerable and heavy losses were inflicted on the enemy far exceeding our own.

ACTION OF THE ENEMY.

1. ARTILLERY.
Co-operation between enemy artillery, Infantry and air was perfect. All calibres up to 15" were fired. *+ Gas*
A very heavy Barrage was put down on CAMBRAI Road end and lifted in accordance with their advance and finally rested on BOURLON WOOD-CAMBRAI ROAD. F.14.d., F.26.a.& b. and F.21.a.& b.

2. INFANTRY.
Assembled in twos and threes for some hours in same manner as at YPRES.
The timing of advance on both flanks was perfect.
The advance was made in 5 waves extended to about 5 paces and about 10 yards interval. A great number of Officers directed the advance and lines were beautifully kept.
The advance was maintained regardless of casualties, on the left within bombing distance of our front line.

The idea was apparently to encircle the village from CAMBRAI and BOURLON WOOD as shown by arrows, with a holding attack on village from the North.

3. Enemy appeared in the village before the line was broken and shot from the Church and Houses in the vicinity.

J. Methuen Lt. Col.
Comdg 4/Seaforth Hrs.

MEDICAL.

50 Bearers were promised to each Battalion.

None however arrived.

Our own Stretchers had to be used to carry down urgent cases on the 21st. inst. These were carried down by prisoners who were stopped on the road.

The Medical Officer sent an Orderly back from LA.JUSTICE on arrival of the Battalion there to find out position of relay post in order to obtain Bearers and Stretchers . The Orderly was unable to find it and went to the Advanced Dressing Station.
They could promise no help at the time and apparently no relay Post had been established. Our own wounded had to be brought down in waterproof sheets and remain till early in the evening of the 22nd. inst. when an Ambulance arrived and started to relieve the great congestion of badly wounded.

CAVALRY.

A Squadron of the Bays arrived at LA JUSTICE on the afternoon of the 21st. inst.

The Squadron Commander agreed to advance through the CANTAING Line after its capture.
Unfortunately just as he was preparing to advance a direct Order arrived for him to take over a portion of the Line about CANTAING. Had he acted as arranged he could have gathered all the Germans running from the CANTAING Line and materially helped in the capture of FONTAINE.

SIGNALS.

The Battalion Signalling Officer had to lay all lines from Brigade Headquarters. He laid a line from FLESQUIERES to LA JUSTICE on 21st inst., helped for a short period by Brigade.
On 22nd. he had to go all the way back from FONTAINE to FLESQUIERES to get wire and pigeons.

CAVALRY.

A Squadron of the Bays arrived at LA JUSTICE on the afternoon of the 21st. inst.

The Squadron Commander agreed to advance through the CANTAING Line after its capture.
Unfortunately just as he was preparing to advance a direct Order arrived for him to take over a portion of the Line about CANTAING. Had he acted as arranged he could have gathered all the Germans running from the CANTAING Line and materially helped in the capture of FONTAINE.

SIGNALS.

The Battalion Signalling Officer had to lay all lines from Brigade Headquarters. He laid a line from FLESQUIERES to LA JUSTICE on 21st inst., helped for a short period by Brigade.
On 22nd. he had to go all the way back from FONTAINE to FLESQUIER to get wire and pigeons.

CAVALRY.

A Squadron of the Bays arrived at LA JUSTICE on the afternoon of the 21st. inst.

The Squadron Commander agreed to advance through the CANTAING Line after its capture.
Unfortunately just as he was preparing to advance a direct Order arrived for him to take over a portion of the Line about CANTAING. Had he acted as arranged he could have gathered all the Germans running from the CANTAING Line and materially helped in the capture of FONTAINE.

SIGNALS.

The Battalion Signalling Officer had to lay all lines from Brigade Headquarters. He laid a line from FLESQUIERES to LA JUSTICE on 21st inst., helped for a short period by Brigade.
On 22nd. he had to go all the way back from FONTAINE to FLESQUIERES to get wire and pigeons.

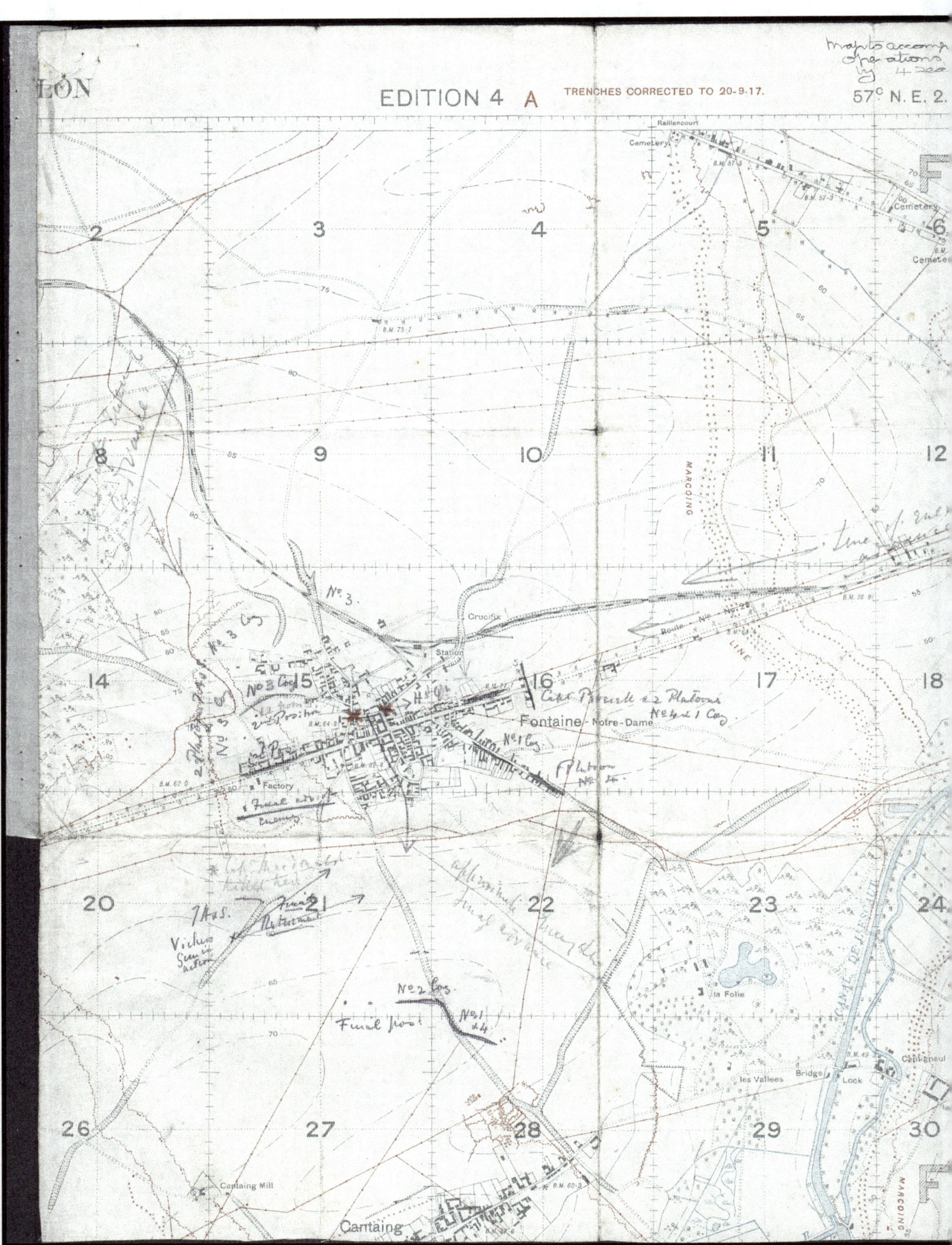

Bassin de radoub	Dry dock.
Bateau phare	Light-ship.
Blanchisserie	Laundry.
B.M. (borne milliaire)	Mile stone.
Bᵏ (borne kilométrique)	
Boulonnerie / Fabᵉ de boulons	Bolt Factory.
Bouée	Buoy.
Brasserie, Brassⁱᵉ	Brewery.
Briqueterie, Briqⁱᵉ	Brickfield.
Brise-lames	Breakwater.
Bureau de poste	Post office.
„ de douane	Custom house.
Butte	Butt, Mound.
Cabane	Hut.
Cabaret, Cabᵗ	Inn.
Câble sous-marin	Submarine cable.
Calvaire, Calvᵉ	Calvary.
Canal de dessèchement	Drainage canal.
Canal d'irrigation	Irrigation canal.
Fabᵉ de caoutchouc	Rubber factory.
Carrière, Carrᵉ	Quarry.
„ de gravier	Gravel-pit.
Caserne	Barracks.
Champ de courses	Race-course.
„ „ manœuvres	Drill-ground.
„ „ tir	Rifle range.
Chantier	Building yard. / Ship yard. / Dock yard.
Chantier de construction	Slip-way.
Chapelle, Chᵉˡˡᵉ	Chapel.
Charbonnage	Colliery.
Château d'eau	Water tower.
Chaussée	Causeway. / Highway.
Chemin de fer	Railway.
Cheminée, Chᵉᵉ	Chimney.
Chêne	Oak tree.
Cimetière, Cimʳᵉ	Cemetery.
Clocher	Belfry.
Clouterie	Nail factory.
Colombier	Dove-cot.
Coron	Workmen's dwellings.
Cour des marchandises / aux dises	Goods yard.
Couvent	Convent.
Crassier	Slag heap.
Croix	Cross.
Darse	Inner dock.
Démoli - e	Destroyed.
Détruit - e, Détᵗ	
Déversoir	Weir.
Digue	Dyke, causeway.
Distillerie, Distⁱᵉ	Distillery.
Douane / Bureau de douane	Custom-house.
Entrepôt de douane	Custom warehouse.
Dynamitière, Dynamᵗᵉ	Dynamite magazine.
Dynamiterie	Dynamite factory.
Écluse	Sluice, Lock.
Éclusette, Eclᵗᵉ	Sluice.
École	School.
Écurie	Stable.
Église	Church.
Émaillerie	Enamel works.
Embarcadère, Embʳᵉ	Landing-place.
Estaminet, Estamᵗ	Inn.
Étang	Pond.
Fabrique, Fabᵉ	Factory.
Fabᵉ de produits chimiques	Chemical works.
Fabᵉ de faïence / Faïencerie	Pottery.
Ferme, Fᵐᵉ	Farm.
Filature, Filʳᵉ	Spinning mill.
Fonderie, Fondⁱᵉ	Foundry.
Fontaine, Fontⁿᵉ	Spring, fountain.
Forêt	Forest.
Forme de radoub	Dry dock.
Forge	Smithy.
Fosse	Mine, Pit.
Fossé	Moat, Ditch.
Four	Kiln.
„ à chaux	Lime-kiln.
Four à coke	Coke oven.
Ganterie	Glove Factory.
Gare	Station.
Garenne	Warren.
Garnison	Garrison.
Gazomètre	Gasometer.
Glacerie / Fabᵉ de glaces	Mirror Factory.
Glacière	Ice factory.
Grue	Crane.
Gué	Ford.
Guérite	Sentry-box, Turret.
„ à signaux	Signal-box (Ry.)
Halte	Halt.
Hangar	Shed, Hangar.
Hôpital	Hospital.
Hôtel-de-Ville	Town hall.
Houillère	Colliery.
Huilerie	Oil factory.
Imprimerie, Imprⁱᵉ	Printing works.
Jetée	Pier.
Laminerie	Rolling mills.
Ligne de haute marée	High water mark.
„ de basse marée	Low „ „
Maison Forestière / Mᵒⁿ Fʳᵉ	Forester's house.
Malterie	Malt-house.
Marbrerie	Marble works.
Marais	Marsh.
Marais salant	Saltern, Salt marsh.
Marché	Market.
Mare	Pool.
Meule	Rick.
Minière	Mine.
Monastère	Monastery.
Moulin, Mⁱⁿ	Mill.
„ à vapeur	Steam mill.
Mur	Wall.
„ crénelé	Loop-holed wall.

Vol 27

Confidential

1/4th Bn. Seaforth Highlanders

War Diary

from 1st December, 1914.
to 31st December, 1914.

Vol. 39

WAR DIARY
or
INTELLIGENCE SUMMARY.
(Erase heading not required.)

Army Form C. 2118.

Volume 39.

Place	Date	Hour	Summary of Events and Information	Remarks and references to Appendices
BAPAUME	1/12/17		Battalion detrained at Bapaume, and marched to Fremicourt arriving there about 5.30 a.m. Marched off again at 10 a.m. to shelters in BERTINCOURT.	m.f
BERTINCOURT	2/12/17		Battalion moved from BERTINCOURT at 1.30 p.m. up to the old British front line. Transport moved to LEBUCQUIERE.	m.f
In the trenches	3/12/17	5.30 p.m.	Battalion moved from old British front line to relieve a Brigade of the 2nd. Division in the front line. (Hindenburg Line) Several casualties on the way up both by M.G. and Shell fire, especially where the trench joined the Cambrai Road. Capt. E.A.Y. Green (Ch.O.) was wounded by shrapnel at that point.	m.f
	4/12/17		About 3.30 p.m. the enemy tried to rush one of our positions between Nos. 3 & 4 Coys. No. 3 Company sent up the S.O.S. signal, and the enemy got caught in our barrage and suffered severe casualties. From this time on until about 9 p.m. our own and enemy artillery were very active. Battalion ordered to evacuate the Hindenburg Line and withdraw carrying as much stores as possible. Lewis Gun teams were left to cover this movement. The 152nd. Brigade took up positions in the old British Line. All dug outs were destroyed before evacuation.	m.f
FREMICOURT	5/12/17		Battalion marched back to huts at FREMICOURT. Artillery very active on both sides. One or two shells dropped on the Cambrai Road.	m.f
	6/12/17		Enemy planes dropped bombs about ½ mile from our camp, causing casualties in the 153rd. Brigade.	m.f
	7/12/17		Nothing of importance occurred.	m.f

Army Form C. 2118.

WAR DIARY
or
INTELLIGENCE SUMMARY.

(Erase heading not required.)

Instructions regarding War Diaries and Intelligence Summaries are contained in F. S. Regs., Part II. and the Staff Manual respectively. Title pages will be prepared in manuscript.

Place	Date	Hour	Summary of Events and Information	Remarks and references to Appendices
FREMICOURT	8/12/17		Battalion commenced sandbagging round the huts, for protection against Bombs. Draft of 52 O.R's arrived from Depot/Battalion. M.J	
	9/12/17		Voluntary Church Services. Col. Unthank proceeds on leave. Battalion under 2 hours notice if wanted up the line, as the Boche was expected to attack. M.J	
	10/12/17		Battalion supplied working parties for C.R.E's, D.A.D.O.S. and town Major. M.J	
	11/12/17		Same working parties as yesterday. Very quiet day. M.J	
	12/12/17		At dawn there was a very heavy bombardment, lasting for about 2 hours. M.J	
	13/12/17		Working parties as usual - Quiet day. M.J	
	14/12/17		" " " " M.J	
	15/12/17		Bosche 'planes over camp 7a.m. Ours and enemy aeroplanes busy all day. M.J	
In the Front Line Trenches	16/12/17		Battalion moved up the line. Left Fremicourt 4 p.m. Relieved the 6th Bn. Black Watch on night 16/17 th. M.J	
	17/12/17		Very quiet day. M.J	
			Snow fell during the night. Observation very bad.	
	18/12/17		Quiet day. M.J	
	19/12/17		Patrol of ours ran into a German outpost, about 400 yds from our wire. 2/Lt. E.J. Martin was wounded there by a machine gun bullet and has died of wounds. A very little fog came on during the morning. M.J	
	20/12/17			

Army Form C. 2118.

WAR DIARY
or
INTELLIGENCE SUMMARY.
(Erase heading not required.)

Instructions regarding War Diaries and Intelligence Summaries are contained in F. S. Regs., Part II. and the Staff Manual respectively. Title pages will be prepared in manuscript.

Place	Date	Hour	Summary of Events and Information	Remarks and references to Appendices
In the Front line trenches	22/12/17		Still misty. Artillery more active on both sides. M.f	
	23/12/17		Mist cleared. Relieved by 2 Coys. 5th Gordons, and 2 Coys. 4th. Black Watch. Marched to tents just outside BANCOURT. M.f	
BANCOURT	23/12/17		Enemy 'planes bombed BANCOURT and FREMICOURT about 5.30 p.m. High explosive bombs were used. Only one casualty in the Battn. M.f	
	24/12/17		Quiet day. Battalion digging protective trenches against bombs. M.f	
	25/12/17		"Holiday" granted by the Brigadier-General. M.f	
	26/12/17		Pte. M. Ward tried by F.G.C.M. on a charge of "self inflicted" wounding. M.f	
	27/12/17		Battalion moved up to LEBUCQUIERE. Struck camp at BANCOURT. M.f	
LEBUCQUIERE	28/12/17		Billeted in huts in the village. Enemy aeroplane brought down by anti-aircraft guns. M.f	
	29/12/17		Battalion supplied a working party of 40 O.R's for work up the line. M.f	
	30/12/17		Artillery very active early. A bombardment was kept up by our guns for about 1½ hours. Battalion supplied a working party of 2 Officers and 100 O.R's for wiring. M.f	
	31/12/17		Same party supplied for wiring. M.f	

M Johton Major
1/4th Seaforth Hylrs
Cmdg

(Confidential)

War Diary

of

1/4th Battn. Seaforth Highlanders.

Volume 40

from 1st January to 31st January 1918.

Army Form C. 2118.

WAR DIARY
or
INTELLIGENCE SUMMARY.
(Erase heading not required.)

Instructions regarding War Diaries and Intelligence Summaries are contained in F. S. Regs., Part II. and the Staff Manual respectively. Title pages will be prepared in manuscript.

Place	Date	Hour	Summary of Events and Information	Remarks and references to Appendices
LEBUCQUIERE	1/1/18		Battalion in huts at village of LEBUCQUIERE. Enemy aeroplanes very active but flying very high. No working parties. Battn. in Brigade Reserve.	
	2/1/18		Battalion supplied a working party of 6 Officers & 300 men for digging new WALSH SUPPORT Trench	
	3/1/18		No working parties. Baths opened at LEBUCQUIERE, & most of the Battn. got bath.	
	4/1/18	8 a.m	Working party supplied of 1 Officer & 50 other ranks	
		11 "	" " " 1 " & 50 " "	
		4 p.m	" " " 4 " & 200 " "	
	5/1/18	7 a.m	" " " 1 " & 30 " "	
		10 30 "	" " " 1 " & 30 " "	
	6/1/18		Two working parties supplied of 2 Officers & 60 other ranks also 4 Officers & 200 other ranks. A working party of 54 men supplied to work on dugouts. Rain in the evening.	
	7/1/18		Same working parties supplied as yesterday. Brigade was relieved tonight.	
	8/1/18		Working party of 1 Officer & 50 other ranks supplied for wiring BEAUMETZ – VAULX Line. Remainder of Battalion digging "slits".	
	9/1/18		Three working parties supplied. "A" 2 Officers & 60 other ranks, "B" 3 Officers & 150 O.R. "C" 1 Officer & 62 other ranks	
	10/1/18		Same working parties as yesterday. Revolver class for Officers started.	

Army Form C. 2118.

WAR DIARY
or
INTELLIGENCE SUMMARY.
(Erase heading not required.)

Instructions regarding War Diaries and Intelligence Summaries are contained in F. S. Regs., Part II. and the Staff Manual respectively. Title pages will be prepared in manuscript.

Place	Date	Hour	Summary of Events and Information	Remarks and references to Appendices
LEBUCQUIERE	11/1/18		Working parties the same as previous 2 days. Capt. W.L. Irons took over the duties of Acting Adjutant. Capt. H.P.T. Ysbey rejoined the Battalion from England.	
	12/1/18		Usual working parties. Baths.	
	13/1/18		Do. Good weather. Church Parade.	
	14/1/18		Working party of 3 Officers & 150 other ranks. Reorganization of Companies prior to going into the line.	
FRONT LINE TRENCHES DEMICOURT.	15/1/18		The Battn. relieved the 1/5th Q.O.L. Yrs. in the line in front of DEMICOURT. No.4 Company remained at LEBUCQUIÈRE. Trenches in a very bad state. Misty & heavy rain all day.	
	16/1/18		Rain in the morning but cleared up in afternoon. Enemy working parties seen in BOURLON WOOD.	
	17/1/18		Raining again & mud worse than ever. Very quiet day. Battalion had a practice counter attack at "Stand to" in the evening.	
FREMICOURT.	18/1/18		Still raining. Battalion was relieved about 4 pm by 9th Suffolk Regt. & moved back to huts at MIDDLESEX Camp, FREMICOURT.	
COURCELLES LE-COMTE.	19/1/18		The Battalion (less No.4 Coy & men not in the line) entrained at FREMICOURT and detrained at ACHIET-LE-GRAND. Marched from there to huts at COURCELLES-LE-COMTE. No.4 Coy marched all the way by road.	

A5834 Wt. W4973/M687 750,000 8/16 D.D. & L. Ltd. Forms/C.2118/13.

WAR DIARY or INTELLIGENCE SUMMARY

Army Form C. 2118.

Place	Date	Hour	Summary of Events and Information	Remarks and references to Appendices
BELLACOURT	20/1/18		Baths filled in at 8.30 a.m. & marched from COURCELLES to BELLACOURT & went into rest billets there. The Division is in Corps Reserve.	W.D.
	21/1/18		Day devoted to cleaning up & resting. Kit inspections. 4 Officers joined the Battalion. Captn. P.C. Knight, 2 Lts. R.C. Williams, W.L. Forsyth, J.S. Ferguson. Also 48 other ranks reinforcements.	W.D.
	22/1/18		Full day. Specialist classes in Lewis Gun, Bombing & Signalling commenced. All men taught to load and fire the Lewis Gun. Coy. drill & training.	W.D.
	23/1/18		Full day. Specialist classes & training of companies continued. Football & recreation in the afternoon. Baths at BAILLEULVAL used by Battalion.	W.D.
	24/1/18		Bright day. Battalion parade at 9 a.m. Training of Coy. & Specialists. Football league. Inter half Coy. matches played in afternoon.	W.D.
	25/1/18		Good day. Battn. parade & Coy. training. Training of Lewis Gunners. Bombing & Signallers. Football in the afternoon.	W.D.
	26/1/18		Good day. Battalion Route march from 9 a.m to 12.30 p.m. Football in afternoon. Draft of 8 men arrived. A concert was given by the Pipe Band party in the Schoolroom, GROSVILLE.	W.D.
	27/1/18		Sunday. Church Parade. Football in the afternoon. Concert given in the Schoolroom by Pipe Band party. Colonel Unthank was present.	W.D.

WAR DIARY
or
INTELLIGENCE SUMMARY

Army Form C. 2118.

Place	Date	Hour	Summary of Events and Information	Remarks and references to Appendices
BELLACOURT	28/1/18		Bright frosty weather. Baths at BAILLEULVAL. Football matches in afternoon.	WD
	29/1/18		Bright day. Nos. 1, 2 & 3 Coys. practised Counter attack from the scheme. No 4 Coy. on the Rifle range. 2/Lt. T.D.ABEL and 3 men joined Battn.	WD
	30/1/18		Bright frosty weather. Box Respirators of Battn. tested at Brigade Gas chamber. No. 1 Coy. on rifle range. Remainder of Coys. under their own Officers. Football matches in the afternoon.	WD
	31/1/18		Very frosty. Companies at musketry, P.T. & B.F. and Tactical scheme. Officers Riding Class under Capt. Gray. Football in the afternoon. Battn. Boxing Competition in the Schoolroom, GROSVILLE at night.	WD

W L Gray Capt
Comdg 11th Bn John Scott

(Confidential)

War Diary

of

1/4th Battn Seaforth Highrs.

Volume 41

from 1st February 1918
till 28th February 1918.

Army Form C. 2118.

WAR DIARY or INTELLIGENCE SUMMARY

(Erase heading not required.)

Instructions regarding War Diaries and Intelligence Summaries are contained in F.S. Regs., Part II. and the Staff Manual respectively. Title Pages will be prepared in manuscript.

Place	Date	Hour	Summary of Events and Information	Remarks and references to Appendices
BELLACOURT	1/2/18		Battn. in rest billets at BELLACOURT. 51st (H)Division in Corps Reserve. Misty cold day. Battn. had baths at BAILLEULVAL. No.1 Coy. at P.T. & B.T. under P.M. Mitchell. No. 3 Coy. on rifle range & Nos. 2 & 4 Coys. at rapid wiring & musketry practice. Football matches in the afternoon. F.& C.	
RITZ Camp near ACHIET LE-GRAND	2/2/18		Cold day. Battn. fell in at 9 a.m. and marched to huts at RITZ camp near ACHIET-LE-GRAND via RANSART, ADINFER, AYETTE & ABLAINZEVILLE. Lt. Col. J. Withand D.S.O. rejoined Battn. from temp. command of 154th Infy. Brigade. Enemy aeroplane came over camp about 1 a.m. but dropped no bombs. F.&.C.	
	3/2/18		Sunday. Bright day but very cold. No Church Parade. Trenches dug round huts & earth banked up round for protection against bombs. Major M. Jobson returned from Aeroplane Course. F.&.C.	
	4/2/18		All day. Training of Coys. in P.T. Gas drill, handling of arms & entrenching musketry. Classes in Lewis Guns, Signalling & Bombing commenced. Lecture given to Officers by Lt. Col. Withand D.S.O. on "The method of advancing for the Counter Attack." Major Jobson went on leave. F.&.C.	
	5/2/18		Bright weather. Training of Companies & Specialists as usual. 2nd Lt. E.T.HATHWAY & 9 O.R. joined Battn. F.&.C.	

WAR DIARY
or
INTELLIGENCE SUMMARY

Army Form C. 2118.

Place	Date	Hour	Summary of Events and Information	Remarks and references to Appendices
Ritz Camp near ACHIET LE-GRAND	7/2/18		Fine day. Coys digging tunnels made huts for protection against bombing. Inter platoon competition in musketry. Winning Rugger 9 Pratt in the afternoon. 2Lt A.G. ROBERTS went on duty to 154 Trench mortar Battery. 9th Royal Scots left the 154th Infantry Brigade to join 11st Division. Battn. attend distinction march on turnip goals from two to one pluce stripe. Capt. J.K. CALDER joined Battn from 5th Army School. P.K.C	
	8/2/18		Full day. Practice attack by Battn on ACHIET-LE-GRAND. No 2 platoon took part in Brigade platoon scheme competition. Digging of shelter trenches made huts continued. P.K.C	
	9/2/18		Wet day. No 11 platoon competed in Brigade platoon musketry competition & took first place. Baths at ABLAINZEVILLE allotted to Battn. Coy 9 Physical training as usual. P.K.C	
	10/2/18		Bright day. Nos. 6 & 11 platoons represented Battn in Brigade march discipline competition & took first place. Naval training of Coys & Specialists. Football match between Battn team 9 No. 49. C.C.S. resulted in 2 goals each. Good day. Battn moved to new camp at LOG EAST WOOD near ABLAINZEVILLE. All men with Battn who came out in 1914 were given free ticket to Divn Theatre.	
LOG EAST WOOD ABLAINZEVILLE	11/2/18		Windy day. Battn attack practice on a village. Lecture by A.P.M. on Field Punishment & by S.G.O.C Division on "method of attack". J.K.C	

Army Form C. 2118.

WAR DIARY or INTELLIGENCE SUMMARY

(Erase heading not required.)

Instructions regarding War Diaries and Intelligence Summaries are contained in F. S. Regs., Part II. and the Staff Manual respectively. Title Pages will be prepared in manuscript.

Place	Date	Hour	Summary of Events and Information	Remarks and references to Appendices
LOQ EAST WOOD	12/2/18		Full day. Battn. attack practice. Football match between 4th Seaforth 9th & 9th.	8.h.S.
ABLAINZEVILLE	13/2/18		Very wet. Battn. marched at 8 a.m. from camp to huts at LEBUCQUIERE via ACHIET-LE-GRAND – BAPAUME – FREMICOURT, about 16 kilometres in 4 hours arriving 12.5 p.m. Battn. in tactical reserve to 152nd Infy. Brigade.	9.h.C.
LEBUCQUIERE	14/2/18		Full day. Cleaning up & resting. 2 hours P.T. & 2 hours Musketry. 2 platoons of Sappers. Mats sent to work on dugouts under 152nd Infy Brigade.	9.h.C.
	15/2/18		Full & cold. Coys at P.T., Musketry, running & new dribbling method of advance.	9.h.C.
	16/2/18		Bright frosty day. Battn. practised alarm in event of attack & took up positions in BEAUMETZ – VAULX line. Enemy aeroplanes came over in the moonlight & dropped bombs.	9.h.C.
	17/2/18		Sunday - Bright cold day. Church service. Enemy aeroplanes again over during night.	9.h.C.
	18/2/18		Cold day. Battn. practised alarm assembly, took up positions. Parties advancing by new dribbling method. Enemy aeroplanes came over during night.	9.h.C.
	19/2/18		Bright frosty day. Coys. at Musketry, Bn. drill & P.T. Piceoluts under their own instructors. Rainy day. Battn. relieved 1/6th Gordon Hrs. in the front line, right sector of the Division (DEMICOURT sector) HQ. No 1 & 4 Coys. in the front line, No 2 Coy. in Support & No 3 Coy. in reserve. Battn. in Durham road near DEMICOURT. 7th Q9 & 10th on left and 17th Division on right. Relief complete by 8.30 p.m. Line very quiet, the enemy line being 1500 – 2000 yards away.	9.h.C.
FRONT LINE TRENCHES N.W. of DEMICOURT	20/2/18			

Army Form C. 2118.

WAR DIARY
or
INTELLIGENCE SUMMARY

(Erase heading not required.)

Instructions regarding War Diaries and Intelligence Summaries are contained in F. S. Regs., Part II. and the Staff Manual respectively. Title Pages will be prepared in manuscript.

Place	Date	Hour	Summary of Events and Information	Remarks and references to Appendices
FRONT LINE TRENCHES N.W. of DEMICOURT.	21/2/18		Bright day but cold. Our aeroplanes were active over enemy lines. Enemy sent a few shells near Battn H.Q. at 9 a.m. Clearing & improving trenches. Carrying party of 50 O.R. supplied to R.E.s. Carrying mine. Front very quiet. Lieut. Dane, Adjutant went on leave & 2 Lt. Q.M.COOPER took over duties of Adjutant. Patrols sent out but no enemy movement seen. P.W.C.	
	22/2/18		Dull day. Line very quiet. Usual working parties. Patrols sent out but no movement seen. P.W.C.	
	23/2/18		Dull day. Enemy & our own artillery fairly active. Our aeroplanes were active. P.W.C.	
	24/2/18		Dull day. Our aeroplanes dropped bombs behind enemy trenches. Enemy shelled near Battn. H.Q. about 3 p.m. P.W.C.	
	25/2/18		Dull day. 9 main. Very quiet on both sides. P.W.C.	
	26/2/18		Bright day. Enemy aeroplanes were active in the morning. Our heavies shelled BOURLON WOOD. Major OSBORNE D.S.O. returned from leave. P.W.C	
	27/2/18		Dull day. Enemy artillery fairly active on villages in rear. Our aeroplanes were active. P.W.C.	
	28/2/18		Cold day. Our heavies were active shelling left edge of BOURLON WOOD. Aeroplanes were active, bombs being dropped by both sides. Line fairly quiet. Major JOBSON rejoined from leave. P.W.C.	

J. Unthank Lt Col.
Commanding
1/4th Bn. Seaforth H'rs

51st Division.
154th Infantry Brigade.

> WAR DIARY

1/4th BATTALION

THE SEAFORTH HIGHLANDERS

MARCH 1918

15W/51

Confidential

War Diary
of
1/4th Battn Seaforth Highlanders.

Volume 42.

from 1st March 1918.
to   31st March 1918.

Army Form C. 2118.

WAR DIARY
or
INTELLIGENCE SUMMARY.
(Erase heading not required.)

Instructions regarding War Diaries and Intelligence Summaries are contained in F. S. Regs., Part II. and the Staff Manual respectively. Title pages will be prepared in manuscript.

Place	Date	Hour	Summary of Events and Information	Remarks and references to Appendices
FRONT LINE TRENCHES N.W. of DEMICOURT	1/3/18		Enemy bombarded trenches on our right at "Stand To". Cold day. A patrol of 1 Off. & 10 men encountered enemy patrol in no Man's Land & were fired on, 1 man being wounded & missing. Our artillery was active during the day.	
	2/3/18		Cold day & snow fall. Line very quiet.	
	3/3/18		Dull day. Observation bad. Line quiet	
	4/3/18		Cold & wet. Observation very poor. Quiet on both sides. Major M. Jobson went to hospital	
	5/3/18		Bright day but windy. Battn. was relieved by 4th Gordon Hrs. in afternoon & went back to huts at Ambulance Camp, LEBUCQUIERE in Brigade Reserve. Casualties during 13 days tour in the front line, 1 O.R. wounded & missing. Working parties supplied every day under R.Es and Pioneers.	
LEBUCQUIERE	6/3/18		Fine day. Resting & cleaning up.	
	7/3/18		Dull day. Battn. boy. training in P.T., musketry, Bombing & drill. Working parties of 3 Officers & 140 O.R. supplied for work under R.Es. Capt. F.W.BROWN joined Battn. from H.Q. 51st (H) Division.	
	8/3/18		Bright day. Training of Coys. Working parties same as yesterday. Battn. relieved 4th Gordon Hrs. in half of night Brigade Sector (DEMICOURT SECTOR) Lt.Col. A.G.I. Hr. taking over from 4th Gordon Hr. in the other half of Brigade Sector.	
	9/3/18		Fine day. Relief complete in daylight. Heavy bombardment on night	

WAR DIARY
INTELLIGENCE SUMMARY
(Erase heading not required.)

Army Form C. 2118.

Place	Date	Hour	Summary of Events and Information	Remarks and references to Appendices
FRONT LINE TRENCHES N.W. of DEMICOURT	10/3/18		Fine day. Visibility poor owing to mist. Line quiet	
	11/3/18		Fine day but misty. Aeroplanes active all day. Enemy shelled BOURSIES and DEMICOURT. R.E.s fired Gas Projectors on enemy trenches on right division (17th Div.) at 4 am. Working parties supplied clearing trenches & sunken roads.	
	12/3/18		Day fine & warm. Large numbers of enemy seen in front of BOURLON WOOD, evidently a relief. Our aeroplanes were active, and enemy aeroplane being engaged & brought down near DOIGNIES.	
	13/3/18		Fine day. Our heavy guns fired an S.O.S. lines from 4 a.m. to 6 a.m. Artillery active on both sides from 2 a.m. to 3 a.m.	
	14/3/18		Dull day & foggy. Artillery quiet. Weather improved later in the day. Artillery quiet. Aeroplanes active on both sides. Battn. relieved by 4th Gordon Hrs. & went back to huts in LEBUCQUIERE.	
LEBUCQUIERE	15/3/18		Fine day. Battn. cleaning up.	
	16/3/18		Fine day. Church parade. Battn. Lt. Col. J. I. Worthand left the Battn. for 6 months tour of duty after having commanded the Battn. for 2 years. Major H.P.D. OSBORNE D.S.O. Middlesex Regt. took over temporary command. Capt. Knight & 4 Lewis gun sections from Battn. left for Divn. Lewis Gun Course.	

Army Form C. 2118.

WAR DIARY
or
INTELLIGENCE SUMMARY.
(Erase heading not required.)

Instructions regarding War Diaries and Intelligence Summaries are contained in F. S. Regs., Part II. and the Staff Manual respectively. Title pages will be prepared in manuscript.

Place	Date	Hour	Summary of Events and Information	Remarks and references to Appendices
LEBUCQUIERE	18/3/18		Fine day. Training of Coys. & Thorolite. Major H.P.D. OSBORNE DSO left Battn. to take over command of K.S.L.I. Lt. Quin. Lt. J.S. HARRIS joined Bn. from 9th Seaforth. 4m. 15 OR Working Party of 1 Off. & 50 OR. 1 Off. & 160 OR working on BEAUMETZ - MORCHIES line	
	19/3/18		Heavy rain. Training of Coys. & Thorolate as usual.	
			Rain in the morning & dull during day. Coys. digging trenches inside huts. Capt. A.M.C. FINCH and Lieut. D. ROSS left Battn. for 6 months duty at home. Major A.C. MACINTYRE 2nd. Lt. A. & S.H. took over temp. command of Battn.	
	20/3/18		Reference MOEUVRES & period sheet 1/20,000 Battn. in Brigade Reserve at LEBUCQUIERE 157 & 153 Infantry Brigade on right, 176th Inf. Bde on left. 19th Div. on right	
	21/3/18	5 a.m.	Enemy shelled village & district very heavily at 5 a.m. with gas shell, HE & shrapnel obtaining direct hit on Battn. HQ.	
		6 a.m.	Battn. ordered to move to position in BEAUMETZ - MORCHIES line	
			BEAUMETZ - MORCHIES line heavily shelled. Major A.C. MACINTYRE (in command) wounded. Capt. H.P.T. GRAY took over command. Troops on left reported retiring. BEAUMETZ - MORCHIES line shelled at intervals of 4 hours during the day.	
		4.15 p.m.	Tanks supported by 2 Battns. of 19th Division advanced through our line to counter attack. Tanks returned about 8.30 pm, also some Infantry. The 19th Div. established 2 posts near BEAUMETZ - DOIGNIES Road. Defensive flanks were thrown out from BRUNO MILL to strong point at J.11.b.9.9 with outpost line in J.22.b.9.d. Night passed quietly.	

WAR DIARY or INTELLIGENCE SUMMARY

Army Form C. 2118.

Place	Date	Hour	Summary of Events and Information	Remarks and references to Appendices
BEAUMETZ - MORCHIES LINE	22/3/18		BEAUMETZ-MORCHIES line heavily shelled. Enemy attacked our front on three occasions. 1 at 10 a.m. 2 at 12.30 p.m. 3 at 3 p.m. & on each occasion was repulsed by our rifle & M.G. fire, leaving many dead on our wire. Artillery support was good on second occasion. Our posts in front of BEAUMETZ-MORCHIES line were forced to withdraw during first attack, the two Officers in command being killed. Ecaps in wire were filled in during the night. One German who came near our wire was captured & another who was on patrol was also captured during the night.	
	23/3/18		Enemy very active. He was seen advancing in masses in LOUVERVAL RIDGE and in valley T.10.c.9.d. – T.9.6.9.d. and in Sunken Road T.15.a.9.b. Artillery action was called for by carrier pigeon but was unanswered. A strong attack was launched on our left about 8.30 a.m. Troops on our left were seen retiring in direction of road in T.20.b. Enemy attacked again on our left Coy. front about 9.5 a.m. He was held up by M.G. & rifle fire until about 10.40 a.m. when a portion of the BEAUMETZ-MORCHIES line was evacuated up to T.21.d.8.9. (Remainder of ¼ No 3 Coy held out line at T.21.a.b. until 3 p.m.) Enemy again advancing on both flanks. A defensive flank formed on our left to link up with WARWICKS up to T.27.c.1.9. Many casualties were inflicted by formation of this flank. Troops seen retiring on both flanks.	

A5834 Wt. W.4973/M687 750,000 8/16 D. D. & L. Ltd. Forms/C.2118/13.

WAR DIARY or INTELLIGENCE SUMMARY

Place	Date	Hour	Summary of Events and Information	Remarks and references to Appendices
BEAUMETZ - MORCHIES LINE	23/3/18		Enemy advancing to VELU WOOD and HERMIES. Enemy in overwhelming numbers all round to Machine gun posted at T.21.a.1.9. enfiladed our trench and inflicted many casualties. Enemy brought up light batteries of field guns which were placed in position in J.15.c.9.d. & fired point blank at our trench. About 3 p.m. enemy entered our trench. It was held for a time but made progress owing to bombs of which we had not a sufficient supply. More of the enemy threatened to enter trench from all sides. It was decided to withdraw to supporting troops on railway behind. On arrival, it was found that all troops had evacuated positions. The WARWICKS were forming a line facing VELU WOOD.	
	24/3/18		A position was taken up at about 10.30 a.m. to the N.E. of the reservoir on the BAPAUME - PERONNE Road about N.5.b. Orders were received about noon to move to the South end of RIENCOURT and form a defensive flank facing East. A ridge had position was taken up on the high ground south of RIENCOURT in support to the 152nd & 153rd Infy. Brigade. About 2 p.m. the enemy were observed debouching from HAPLINCOURT WOOD. At the same time large bodies of troops were reported to be retiring from the direction of LE TRANSLOY. This retirement continued throughout the afternoon.	

WAR DIARY
or
~~INTELLIGENCE SUMMARY~~
(Erase heading not required.)

Army Form C. 2118.

Place	Date	Hour	Summary of Events and Information	Remarks and references to Appendices
N E of BAPAUME – PERONNE Rd about N.5 b.	24/3/18	3 p.m.	Orders were received about 3 p.m. to cover the retirement of the 152nd Brigade. About 6 p.m. the 152nd Inf. Brigade began to fall back through our lines. Our position was held until dusk, when a gradual retirement with rearguard action began to the West of the BAPAUME – PERONNE Rd. Here another position was taken up on the high ground in N.4.a.9.c. and patrols were sent out to gain touch with the enemy. No enemy was encountered West of the BAPAUME – PERONNE Road. Orders were received about 10.30 p.m. to retire towards THILLOY.	
	25/3/18		The Division was reorganised on the BAPAUME – ALBERT Road and marched to WARLENCOURT – EAUCOURT where shell hole positions were taken up facing East. These positions had just been occupied when word was received that the Brigade on our right had retired to the COURCELETTE line and that enemy patrols were in DELVILLE WOOD. It was decided to form a defensive flank and remain where we were. Authority was given to a sapper of the C.O.R.C.C by the Battn. to destroy MIRAUMONT – THILLOY railway track at 9.30 a.m. From 10.30 a.m. onwards reports of retirements on our left flank were received. The enemy was also observed advancing in large numbers from the direction of LA BARQUE and also over the high ground to the SOUTH WEST. At 11.40 a.m. our front began to retire but men were rallied and returned again to their positions. A number of casualties were inflicted on the enemy who was advancing in large numbers over the ridge near LA BARQUE.	

Army Form C. 2118.

WAR DIARY
or
INTELLIGENCE SUMMARY.
(Erase heading not required.)

Place	Date	Hour	Summary of Events and Information	Remarks and references to Appendices
WARLENCOURT EAUCOURT	25/3/18		About 12 noon we were fired on heavily from the rear by Machine Guns. Thinking that the enemy had surrounded us it was decided to withdraw & fight our way back to MIRAUMONT. We learnt subsequently that our own Machine Guns had mistaken us for the enemy. About 1 p.m. the enemy was observed to be attempting an enveloping movement from the high ground to the N.W. of COURCELETTE. Orders were received to withdraw to withdraw by easy stages while a defensive flank to our right was thrown out by the 7th. A.& 2 Bn. A new position was eventually taken up by us on the high ground to round PYS and by the 152nd and 9 151st Inf. Brigades on the high ground east of IRLES. The enemy continued his advance — massing for new attacks N. of IRLES in LOUPART WOOD on the high ground east and south of PYS. The Battn. took up a position to the S.W. of PYS. about 3.30 p.m. Many casualties were inflicted on the enemy here by rifle & M.G. fire. About 6.30 p.m. the enemy was observed working round both our flanks and a general withdrawal of the Division began in the direction of MIRAUMONT. At COLINCAMPS the Division was reorganised and marched to bivouac near SAILLY au BOIS.	D.D
SAILLY AU BOIS	26/3/18		At dawn on the 26th. an outpost line was thrown out facing S.E. covering SAILLY au BOIS. At 8.30 a.m. orders were received to withdraw to SOUASTRE. new positions were taken up here until relieved by Australians at about 3 p.m.	

WAR DIARY or INTELLIGENCE SUMMARY

Army Form C. 2118.

Place	Date	Hour	Summary of Events and Information	Remarks and references to Appendices
SAILLY AU BOIS	26/3/18		Casualties during operations from 21st – 27th March 1918:-	
			Officers – Killed in action – Capt. J.S.HARRIS , Lieut. J.K.CALDER , 2.Lt. W.L.FORSYTH.	
			Wounded – Major A.C.MACINTYRE (8th A&14th) Cornd'g , Capt. H.P.T.GRAY , 2/Lt. L.S.GANDER 2.Lt. J.N.MACDONALD , 2.Lt. R.G. WILLIAMS.	
			Wounded & Missing – 2.Lt. G.M.COOPER , Capt. F.W.BROWN , Lieut. A.MACRAE	
			Missing – Capt. P.C.KNIGHT , Lieut. J. DAVIDSON , Capt. J.F.HARDESTY (U.S.A.M.C)	
			Sick – 2.Lt. J.CHRISTIE	
			Other Ranks. Killed 29 , Wounded 129 , Wounded & Missing 21,	
			Wounded (gas) 2 , Missing 204 , Sick 17.	
BARLY	28/3/18		Batt. proceeded via DOULLENS to billets at BARLY near DOULLENS. Major M.JOBSON rejoined the Batt. from Hospital & took over command.	
			Lieut. A.G. CAMPBELL joined Batt. from 154 Trench Mortar Battery.	
	28/3/18		Quiet day. Cleaning up & resting.	
BUSNETTES	29/3/18		Batt. marched to FREVENT Station & entrained about 6 p.m. , arriving at LILLERS about 12 midnight. Marched from LILLERS to billets at BUSNETTES.	

A5834 Wt. W4973/M687 750,000 8/16 D.D. & L. Ltd. Forms/C.2118/13.

Army Form C. 2118.

WAR DIARY
or
INTELLIGENCE SUMMARY.
(Erase heading not required.)

Place	Date	Hour	Summary of Events and Information	Remarks and references to Appendices
BUSNETTES	30/3/18		Wet day. Resting & cleaning up.	
	31/3/18		Fine day. Baths. Church Parades.	